THE ORIENTAL ANNUAL

CONTAINING A SERIES OF

TALES, LEGENDS, & HISTORICAL ROMANCES

THE ORIENTAL ANNUAL

CONTAINING A SERIES OF

TALES, LEGENDS, & HISTORICAL ROMANCES

BY

THOMAS BACON, ESQ., F.S.A.

AUTHOR OF "FIRST IMPRESSIONS, AND STUDIES FROM NATURE IN HINDOSTAN," ETC. ETC.

WITH
ENGRAVINGS BY W. AND E. FINDEN,
FROM
SKETCHES BY THE AUTHOR;
AND
CAPTAIN MEADOWS TAYLOR,
OF THE SERVICE OF HIS HIGHNESS THE NIZAM.

GYAN

Published by

GYAN

Gyan Publishing House
5, Ansari Road
Daryaganj, New Delhi-110002
Phone: 011-47034999, 9811692060
E-mail: books@gyanbooks.com

Distribution Network
gyanbooks.com
India, USA, Canada, UK, Australia, France

ISBN : 978-81-212-3853-3 (PB)
First Published, 1840

2nd Impression 2020

Printed at: Gyan Press, Delhi.

THE

ORIENTAL ANNUAL;

CONTAINING A SERIES OF

Tales, Legends, & Historical Romances;

BY

THOMAS BACON, Esq., F.S.A.,

AUTHOR OF "FIRST IMPRESSIONS, AND STUDIES FROM NATURE IN HINDOSTAN," ETC, ETC.

WITH

ENGRAVINGS BY W. AND E. FINDEN,

FROM

SKETCHES BY THE AUTHOR;

AND

CAPTAIN MEADOWS TAYLOR,

OF THE SERVICE OF HIS HIGHNESS THE IZAM.

LONDON:

CHARLES TILT, FLEET STREET.

1840.

[illegible]

Drawn by H. Warren from a Sketch by Capt. Meadows Taylor. Engraved by Finden.

[illegible]

London, Published Oct 1 1839 by Charles Tilt, 86 Fleet Street.

ADDRESS.

The "fearful boldness" with which the Author committed the last (his first) Volume of The Oriental Annual to publication, has been changed to comfortable confidence by the indulgent and very handsome encouragement bestowed upon him, on all sides. He expects, too, increased favour from the co-operation of his talented friend, Captain Meadows Taylor, who has assisted him, not only with his beautiful Sketches, but also with valuable Notes upon parts of India into which the Author had not travelled.

T. B.

Mount Radford, Exeter,
August 11, 1839.

LIST OF PLATES.

THE

ORIENTAL ANNUAL.

PENKONDA.

No scape of Nature, no distempered day,
No common wind, no customèd event,
But they will pluck away his natural cause,
And call them meteors, prodigies, and signs,
Abortives, présages, and tongues of heaven.

KING JOHN.

In the chain of rocky hills which form the north-east frontier of the kingdom of Mysore there is a *droog* or fortified hill, called Penkonda, remarkable for the boldness of its form and the picturesque beauty of its formation. It is not a little celebrated in the histories of the Mysore and Dekkan dynasties, and contains many fine memorials of their former grandeur. Dilapidated palaces and other architectural remains, both Moslem and Hindoo, are there thrown together in strange confusion; and, in some instances, the most grotesque mixtures of these incongruous styles are found in the same structure, the place having passed from the possession of one power to the other, as each alternately rose and declined.

An ancient palace, called the Ghugun Mahal, exhibits some curious tokens of these reverses. The basement is of plain massive Hindoo construction and of great antiquity, coeval apparently with some temples of Mahadeo which stand near it. The next story is of more recent date, and is built in the best style of Mohummedan architecture, elaborately ornamented, as if the builders had desired that it should form as forcible a contrast as possible with the Hindoo workmanship. Since its erection, again, it is apparent that attempts have been made by the Hindoos to alter the Moslem devices into something which should better assimilate with their own work; the very cupolas have been surmounted with inelegant pyramidical roofs, and a beautiful Saracenic screen, carved in white marble, has been mutilated, and in part replaced by some miserable representations of dragons, and other grotesque fabulous monsters—poor substitutes for the delicate flowers and intricate arabesques, of which a few specimens still remain.

There is, perhaps, but one considerable building in the place which has escaped these motley transformations, and that is by far the most ancient of all. It is the Sunkul-Boorjh, a high irregular bastion near the western gate of the fortress, a view of which is given in the vignette upon the title-page

Drawn by W. Warren, from a Sketch by Capt. Meadows Taylor

The Gungun Mahal Penconda

of this volume. It is said to have been built more than a thousand years since, but the Hindoos affirm that Krishna, having taken it into especial favour, has preserved it throughout from the depredations of time, no less than the attacks of the Mohummedans. It must formerly have stood without the fortifications, and was probably used as a monastery, being laid out in a series of small cells, most miserably dark and dreary, fit only for the habitation of ascetics, or reptiles, and *bhoots.**

The gateway shown in the drawing, near the salient angle of the lower rampart, is also of Hindoo origin; though here, too, the officious handiwork of the Moslems is conspicuous, the venerable pile being overlaid with a complication of Saracenic decorations, in lamentable discordance with the solemn style of its architecture. Having been once a grand impressive structure, it now presents a ludicrous laughing-crying effect, not at all unlikely to impose a fit of hysterics upon any lady beholder of common susceptibility. It is unquestionably more ancient than the surrounding ramparts; although, it is impossible to assign an exact date to any building in Penkonda, owing to the deficiency of antiquarian statistical lore among the inhabitants, who acknowledge a decided preference for the mystic vagaries of

* A family of the spirits of darkness, delighting in pestilential vaults, damp-stained, and honey-combed by the tooth of time.

tradition over the precise truths of history. No better evidence of this predilection could be given than their eagerness to relate to every enquiring visitor their favourite

LEGEND OF FAKHIR-UD-DEEN,

which very ingeniously, to say the least of it, accounts for that strange admixture of the Mohummedan and Hindoo orders of architecture, from which the city derives so peculiar a character. I shall tell the tale, as nearly as possible, in the words of the narrators.

In the early part of the thirteenth century, these provinces, which were then in the highest state of agricultural and commercial prosperity, were invaded by the enterprising and insatiable Moguls. The Hindoo sovereign, Hari Raial, who held his court at Viziernuggur, was attacked and driven from his capital; and, retreating with a few followers for several days, while the enemy were engaged in pillaging his treasures, he escaped unnoticed to a remote mountain. Finding the place almost impregnable by nature, he speedily built and fortified a city, which was considered capable of setting at defiance all the military skill and power of the invaders. In this spot he remained many years unmolested; and as he was a warm patron of the arts, and had some ambition to be well spoken of by posterity, he built many handsome edifices, and a magnificent palace, which he proudly styled the Ghugun Mahal, the Palace of the Sky. Yet the memory of his former capital and all his lost wealth never forsook him, and, as his years increased, his enmity against his former despoilers was strengthened: so that, when his spirit was about to be absorbed into the essence of Brahma, he imposed a solemn injunction upon his son, Drooghi Raial, that he should never suffer a Moslem to enter the gates of the city, under any circumstances either of peace or of war. Drooghi Raial was filled with pious enthusiasm, and, immediately on the death of his father, issued a wise and sacred edict, announcing that if any of his subjects should admit a Mussulman to the city, or finding him already there, should omit to slay him, or should, either wittingly or in ignorance, assist or befriend a Mussulman, he should, even upon slender testimony thereof, be instantly condemned to a death of extreme torture.

In these times, Penkonda was blessed by the favour and countenance of a most sanctified Brahmin, whose humble abode was upon the sacred hill of Pennakoel, on the east side of the city. One morning, while this venerable man was engaged in his usual religious exercises, he became so absorbed in devotion that he did not notice the approach of a stranger, leading a cow, until his blood spontaneously curdled; and, on seeking the cause of his disorder, he beheld a man, at no great distance, who having just slain a cow, was then preparing to satiate his diabolical appetite upon its sacred flesh. Appalled and disgusted at this horrible sacrilege, the pious Brahmin fled, with all practicable speed, to the Ghugun Mahal, where Drooghi Raial was then presiding in the Hall of Justice; having waited a second to collect a few atoms of his dispersed breath and wits, just sufficient to make himself understood, he spread terror and dismay among the assembly, by his awful tale. "Alas! alas!" cried the bewildered Raja, "what complexity of evils will not, from this day forth, attend upon the very name of Penkonda? Instantly bring hither the vile culprit, and let the precious proofs of his guilt be likewise produced, that we may without the loss of a moment extinguish this *gaubur's* foul existence."

Presently, the armed force, who had spurred to execute the Raja's commands, returned urging before them, at the points of their spears, a tall and remarkably graceful person, of handsome countenance and noble strength, who betrayed neither fear nor excitement. The head and legs of the cow were also, with every demonstration of the greatest veneration, brought into the Justice Hall.

"Foul dog! execrable reptile!" cried the enraged Raja; "speak, and declare how thy unhappy parents have called thee, that thy hateful name may descend a thousand generations, to be loathed and accursed among the future inhabitants of Penkonda. Speak, dog; but not with a vain hope to save thy abhorred life; for I see that, if not an utter infidel, thou'rt worse,—a follower of the false Prophet of Ishmael; and, therefore, thy doom is sealed. Speak quickly, thou most loathsome descendant of a race of pigs!"

The Moslem was unmoved by the Raja's rage, and smiling calmly, he replied—"My name, most respectable Drooghi Raial, is Fakhir-ud-Deen. I am a devout worshipper of the true God, whose prophet is Mohummed. If you would put your mistaken faith in competition with that for which I am ever ready to die, if you would distinguish between darkness and light, command yon vaunting priest of Pennakoel to give life and proportion to these scattered bones and sinews."

"Wretch!" screamed the incensed Raja, "dost thou dare to ridicule our sacred things, and pour contempt upon the holy Brahmin? Of what use are these remnants of thy impious feast, without the breathing life?"

"Good Drooghi Raial," replied the stranger, "restrain thy impotent wrath; and, if you would behold truth, be pleased to command your extraordinary priest to do what I have named."

Hereupon the reproved Raja enquired of the Brahmin if he could perform the required miracle; and the Brahmin replied, that one little obstacle alone prevented the accomplishment of the animal's resuscitation; this was the simple circumstance, that the members would become corrupt ere the long prayers and religious rites necessary on the occasion could be repeated and performed. The stranger, with a placid look of triumph, now began to repeat a few sentences in Arabic. As he proceeded in his incantations the shattered limbs began to grow apace, and having presently united, formed a cow precisely similar to that which had been slain, to the complete astonishment and dismay of all beholders. Not less than the rest of those present, the king was astounded, as he saw this animal, not only with all the appearance, but having all the functions, of an ordinary cow. Yet the force of his mind restraining all unseemly exhibition of his feelings, he soon recovered from his unbecoming surprise, and thus addressed the mysterious stranger.

"Truly, my friend, thou art an expert conjuror, and hast evidently too close a connexion with the spirits of darkness; but since thy boasted truth is worthy of trial, and likewise for the glory of the great Brahma, whose power will assuredly triumph, I shall immediately cause thee, and that venerable Brahmin, to be sown up each in a sack of lime, and to be cast into the deep waters of the reservoir. Then will the true God stretch forth his right arm, and rescue him who is devoid of guile."

The sentence here pronounced was forthwith executed upon the two devotees, despite the remonstrances of the Brahmin; and no sooner had the sack in which the stranger was confined sunk beneath the surface of the water, than the opposite holy hill of Pennakoel resounded with loud cries of "*La illa oola Mohummed Russool oola,*" and the handsome form of the Mohummedan was seen performing genuflexions on the terrace of the Brahminical temple; but the aged Brahmin sank, and was never more heard of. Having beheld this wonderful exhibition of the supreme truth of the God of Ishmael, Drooghi Raial, and all his court, and all the inhabitants of Penkonda, even to the youngest babe, became immediate converts to Mohummedism, more zealous even than those who had been born and nurtured in the faith. Not only did they, one and all, by inspiration, utter the truths of their new creed like true and experienced Moslems, but, though insensibly, their ideas and actions became in all things suitable. Thenceforth, all their architects, artificers, and cunning workmen, devised and wrought with the minds and hands of Moslems, as may be seen by the style of all masonry since that day.

There yet remains to be told, that from the moment of the Mohummedan's immersion and miraculous rescue, the waters of the reservoir became milk of the most delicious kind, such as the Prophet has promised shall be ever flowing for the use of the blessed in the stream of the second river of Paradise; and it is credibly reported among the Faithful, that its supernatural qualities continued unimpaired, until affected by the religious degeneracy of the inhabitants. Alas! who can behold unmoved the utter prostration of its present people? Alas! Alas! those broad waters, though still white to the eye, retain no property more lacteous than may be supposed to result from the solution of the two sacks of lime. Yet, is it to be expected that an atom of humanity can exalt itself to the stirrup-tassels of the sun, or a moth fly over the battlements of the heavens?

It will probably add not a little to the reader's interest in this legend, that all the localities alluded to are to be recognised in the accompanying views of the place.

It was to this fortress that Ram Raja of Bijanuggur fled for refuge from the combined forces of the Mohummedan sovereigns of the Dekkan, after the total rout of his army on the plains of Talicotta. Here he collected the few remnants of his troops, the mere wreck of his once gallant bands; and, setting out for Bijanuggur, endured a painful and harassing march, only to find his capital plundered and deserted. The grief of Ram Raja on meeting with this new calamity was so excessive, that, although in the prime of life, his face was bowed to the earth with affliction, and he shortly died of a broken heart. His successor abandoned the capital, and, with the small remnant of power left in his hands, removed his diminished court, and the seat of government, to Penkonda; where, owing, in all probability, to his insignificance, he remained unmolested, throughout many successive revolutions in the Dekkan and the surrounding kingdoms, until the middle of the seventeenth century.

The Hindoo temples in Penkonda are still occasionally made use of, as places of worship; though, I believe, the mixed tombs of Mohummedan and Hindoo saints, upon the high rocks beyond the town, appear to be more highly venerated. In the temple which is devoted to the worship of the *lingam*, a perpetual light has been kept burning before the altar, as the Brahmins affirm, ever since the edifice was completed,—a period of, at least, four centuries.

The inhabitants of Penkonda and its vicinity are peculiarly simple-hearted, and in every way most primitive in their manners and ideas. They are altogether devoid of that low cunning which I have always found inseparable from the Hindoo character, and though equally superstitious with the rest of their fellows, they exhibit no sort of bigotry or ill-feeling towards the Mohummedan or Christian faith; assuming that all should be true to the religion in which they are born, as the service most acceptable to the Deity. It is said by the priests that in this place arose the custom, now common in India, of considering that he who bestows, not he who receives, charity is the party favoured. Thus in giving alms, they thank the person who receives their money, and the latter usually replies that they are welcome to his goodness in accepting their bounty. Their method of avenging themselves upon an aggressor is truly absurd. They drive an ass to the threshold of their enemy's house, and there slay it; by which act the house is polluted beyond remedy, and the family are obliged immediately to desert it. Should any of them remain under the roof until the blood be cooled, they cannot be purified except by a long and annoying series of ceremonies, and at much expense.

The mosque of Shere Shah is perhaps the handsomest building in Penkonda, and if erected by the chief whose name it bears, must be nearly three hundred years old. It is of a dark grey granite, with mouldings of a jet-black stone resembling hornblend, wrought with all the nicety and skill of Oriental masonry. Behind this mosque, the hill rises precipitously to the height of five or six hundred feet; presenting a rugged and apparently inaccessible face, partially overgrown with ragged bushes and jungul, from which sharp angles of rock project in all directions. In other places, again, there is not a blade of vegetation to be seen, and the naked rocks lie piled heap upon heap, with here and there, perched on some giddy point, a tomb, an altar, or a line of battlements, without an indication of the path by which it is to be approached. Upon the top of the mountain, embedded between two fantastic peaks, is the citadel, a ponderous mass of masonry, which looks as if by its weight it had cloven the summit asunder, and was now about to sink into the earth. Within the walls of this elevated retreat, are the remains of several palaces and temples, and the scenery around is wild and desolate, dark, rugged and uncultivated; but there is a grandeur about it which is wonderfully imposing, an air of mystery and gloom, a howling solitude, which render it a proper cradle for the scolding winds, threatening clouds, and fire-dropping storms. A home it is

> ——Wherein the cub-drawn bear would couch,
> The lion, and the belly-pinched wolf,
> Keep their fur dry.

It was in these regions of desolation and waste, that the army of the renowned Mallek-ul-Tija was destroyed by a petty raja, named Sirkeh, in the time of Miamun Oolla, who was Suba of the district, about the middle of the fifteenth century. The tale is known under the title of

SIRKEH'S REVENGE,

and is thus told:—

MALLEK-UL-TIJA, with a very large army, invested

a certain hill-fort, the capital of Raja Sirkeh, carried it by storm, and took Sirkeh prisoner. Having pillaged the fort, the conqueror promised to spare the life of the unfortunate Raja, if he would embrace the Moslem faith; but he, being a devout Hindoo, took some pains to consider how he might avoid apostacy, and yet preserve his head. Being gifted with a subtle wit, a smooth tongue, and much duplicity of manner, he speedily contrived and executed a plan, which not only restored him to liberty, but enabled him to enjoy a savage revenge upon his enemy. Consummate coolness and address were necessary for the success of the Raja's plot; but being master of the three valuable qualities above-mentioned, he was not likely to lack confidence. After inducing Mallek-ul-Tija to believe that the force of his arguments rather than the fear of death, —for Sirkeh was known to be a brave man,—had well nigh made him a convert to Mohummedism, the Raja persuaded his tyrannical captor that he had now but one difficulty remaining in his mind; and that, from the natural pride of his heart, he feared this one obstacle to his conversion would be insuperable; so he pretended that he should prefer to resign his life at once, rather than, in a manner unbecoming the decision of character for which he was so greatly admired, continue in doubt and suspense. "Most potent Mallek," said he, "about forty miles distant from hence, in an almost impregnable fort, surrounded with a difficult and thickly-populated country, there lives a Raja, by name Sanghir, whom I regard as my natural enemy, whose forefathers my forefathers, since the day of Abraham, have regarded as their natural enemy. Now if, for conscience' sake, I shall become a disciple of the divine prophet, so long as my enemy Sanghir continues upon his *musnud*, he will not cease to point the finger of scorn and derision at my altered turban; the blistering lash of his tongue will be extended and strengthened; he will make the change of my faith, hearty and conscientious though it be, a handle for his evil influence; he will not cease his clamorous mockery, until he has urged my family and subjects into open rebellion against me, until he has planted his cursed foot upon my prostrate neck, until his hated hand (may it wither!) has grasped the sceptre of my ancient kingdom, the heir-loom of a thousand generations. Had I not better secure to myself, while it is in my power, the privilege of having my head smitten from my shoulders, by the merciful right arm of the renowned Mallek-ul-Tija?"

Mallek-ul-Tija, blinded by the affected earnestness and humility of the Raja, replied: "Good Sirkeh, if this trifle be the only impediment to your conversion, let it not harass your virtuous mind; I will give orders immediately that with to-morrow's dawn we march upon Sanghir's territory. Although, as you say, it is a difficult country for most travellers, yet to the brave and powerful spirits who compose the army of Malek-ul-Tija, the road will be smooth. Be comforted, then, for by this ruddy sword of my sires I swear that ere the conquering Sun shall have thrice dispersed the starry forces of retreating Night, the standard of Mallek-ul-Tija shall spread its broad shadow over the boasted stronghold of this unbelieving Sanghir. Courage, my friend! I tell you that, while one single follower of Mallek-ul-Tija remains to him, you shall deal bloody stripes of vengeance on this your ill-fated foe; and as a reward for your devotion, you shall receive all the honours of his crest and every *biga* of his dominion; while for my master, the immortal Sultan, I reserve only the contents of the treasury and the personal property of the Raja, with a trifling imposition of tribute, say a hundred *lahks* annually, to be paid simply as a token of your allegiance."

"Bountiful succour of the afflicted," replied the crafty Sirkeh, who in his heart had sworn, with equal warmth, that, ere those three days were accomplished, Mallek-ul-Tija should have gone to meet his vaunted sires; "as your princely heart is o'erflowing with generosity, so is your right hand replete with power. But alas! you know not the dangers, the intricacies, the insuperable obstructions, which throng the narrow passage into those chaotic wildernesses which the vain Sanghir proudly calls a kingdom. Dense forests teeming with all sorts of wild beasts, hanging cliffs, scarped ravines, and intersecting mountain torrents, concealed in treacherous jungul, must be obstacles impracticable even to so godlike an army as that of the invincible Mallek-ul-Tija, without a skilful guide. So impracticable, indeed, are these wilds, and so boundless, that if a million of men were dispersed through them they might wander for ages and no two of them ever meet again; any more than the particles of spray into which a drop of water is shaken in the vast cataract of Gungootri will ever again unite amid the immeasurable waters of the rolling Ganges."

"But is there no guide among your own followers, then, short-sighted Sirkeh? Have your forces so seldom made incursions upon Sanghir's territory, that not a man can be found in your army to thread those devious paths. To the blind, undoubtedly, they will be impassable; but to the wary and long-sighted they will be laid out as upon a map. To the wise and brave nothing is difficult; but even the wise and brave may conform to common usage, and avail themselves of such aid as Providence may cast in their way."

"Great Mallek," said Sirkeh, "you speak indeed the words of wisdom. I have, in my humble retinue, a slave who was born and nurtured in the heart of those dread junguls; who, in the darkest night, or under the blackest rush of the monsoon, would thread his way and guide your highness's army to its destination. He shall be a torch in your hand, and assuredly we shall then easily surmount these difficulties, and pluck the rose of accomplishment, without trouble; and we shall yet see the fulfilment of your excellency's vow. This slave shall precede us, and five thousand of my best soldiers shall follow to behold the downfall of their enemy. Let us set forth, most noble Mallek; I am impatient of delay, now that I see this ray of light which you have cast upon my path."

It was on a beautiful fresh morning in the spring, A. D. 1453, that Mallek-ul-Tija, attended by 500 nobles of Medina, Kurballa, and Nujif, and also with many Dekkani and Abyssinian chiefs, each a hero of a thousand trophies, set forth upon their march towards the dominions of Sanghir. Ten thousand chosen horse, their clashing arms and rattling hoofs greeting the early dawn, their glittering banners spread, and their countless spears waving like corn before the breeze, led by their gallant chief, passed proudly upon their way; now filing through the narrow defile, and now again spreading across the open plain. For many hours, without check or hindrance, they continued their course through a diversified country, here partially cultivated, here deeply shrouded with jungul and forest wood, and there again a waste and trackless plain; so that at high noon, when Mallek-ul-Tija commanded a halt, at the foot of a low range of hills, he, in a bantering tone, bid Sirkeh go and refresh himself after so arduous an excursion; adding, that if he were sufficiently restored from his fatigue after an hour's repose, they would proceed. Sirkeh in silence withdrew, and seating himself at a distance from the Moslem chief, invited his humble follower, the guide, to partake of his repast.

That day, before the sun had set, Mallek-ul-Tija had confessed that the difficulties of the road were even greater than he had anticipated. Indeed, although he and his body-guard, attended by Sirkeh and the guide, had traversed many miles since noon, they were certain that the rear of the line could not have advanced very far from the spot where they had rested, so narrow and irregular had been the pass through which they wound their way. And thus they bivouacked during the night.

Upon the first appearance of returning day, again, the warriors proceeded. It was a chill dull morning, shut in with heavy clouds rolling before a driving wind, unusual at that season; but Mallek-ul-Tija pleasantly observed to Sirkeh, that his minions of wind and water were ordered out to clear the way and lay the dust before his army. For once, however, his humour failed to excite a cordial laugh among his followers; so that the great man stared, and his lips involuntarily muttered "How so?" A forced laugh from the foremost officers answered him; they would have laughed as boisterously as ever, had they been able; but there was a something in the air, a something in the scene, so cold and desolate, that even courtiers could not command a happy laugh. The gloomy feeling which prevailed soon communicated itself to the chief; and as they slowly struggled on through wreathed underwood and hanging boughs, and over broken ground and deep ravines, where the horses could scarcely find footing, the spirit of silence descended upon all; and only now and then a growled oath, a muttered curse, was heard as the fretted steeds floundered and scrambled on, wounding their limbs upon the splintered rocks, and dragging their riders through the tangled thorns. When at noon they again halted, the proud commander with a gloomy frown ordered three hours' rest, instead of one, remarking that, as they must soon be on the borders of Sanghir's territories, they would have their troopers fresh for their march to the capital. Then turning to Sirkeh, he said in the hoarse voice of ill-temper: "Truly, friend Sirkeh, you have kept your promise; and be assured I will also keep mine. So far were you from exaggerating the difficulties of this abominable country, that your words in reality gave me but a faint idea of what my gallant troops would have to encounter. Never could the imaginations of poets have painted to the view paths so horrible. They tell of darkened roads, of pestilent shrouded passes, so thickly strewn with terrors that a male tiger through dread of them would become a female; more full of windings than wreathed snakes, narrower than the bridge to Paradise. But these are trifles to what we have this day passed through."

Yet Mallek-ul-Tija, though chafed at the unexpected obstacles which his army had met with, and the consequent loss of time, and though fretted at having his men scattered so far from his person, knew not yet one half the evils of the country into which he had advanced. His followers soon reported to him that the water was fetid and unfit for use, that when they attempted to light their fires for cooking, the soil itself ignited and burned so fiercely that they feared to set the whole country in flames, and that scorpions, adders, and venomous lizards, swarmed under every stone, in every tuft of grass. Having ascertained the truth of these reports, Mallek-ul-Tija broke forth in bitter curses upon that wretched country, and remounting his jaded charger, gave orders to move forward to some more favoured spot.

Slowly, and with increased difficulty, the foremost of the body-guard made their way through the jungul, breaking down a passage for their chief; but as they fell frequently into concealed ravines, and swamps, and blackened water-courses, by neglecting or mistrusting the directions of the guide, Mallek-ul-Tija found that his best and bravest followers were being sacrificed one by one. He now began to suspect the sincerity of Sirkeh, and ordering the guide to be brought before him, he closely cross-examined him, first as to his master, and next as to the country which lay before them. The guide spoke openly and freely of his master, and with so much tact as entirely to remove Mallek-ul-Tija's suspicions. As to his knowledge of the country, he replied that, in order to prove his truth, he would minutely describe each new difficulty which was yet to be encountered, and, if the chief did not find them precisely as he foretold, then, let his head pay the price of his falsehood. This he acted upon, and Mallek-ul-Tija, as they again advanced, finding the rocks, the river, and the mountain pass, exactly as the guide had predicted, regained a measure of his confidence. Here and there the way became a little more practicable, but still they could not discover a suitable place of repose, owing to the noxious effluvia of the soil, and the swarms of venomous reptiles which infested the ground. The character of the country was, however, becoming more mountainous, and, although the guide would make no flattering promises, Mallek-ul-Tija could not help hoping that they might yet discover some pleasant valley in which to bivouac. Night drew on, however, without any more cheering prospect, and after winding fatigued, alarmed, and spirit-fallen, until it was almost dark, the foremost troops entered a narrow ravine overhung by a dense forest, a passage through which was difficult even to the gale. Demons would have started at the arched precipices and frowning caverns; the *ghole** would have been panic-struck at the sight of them. The sun never enlightened the valleys, nor had Providence thought fit to fix any bounds to their extent. The grass was tough as the teeth of serpents, and the air foul as the breath of dragons. Death dwelt in the waters, and poison was distilled from the trees; the grinning skulls and bleached bones of thousands of travellers lay scattered on all sides. However, there being in this place room for all his troops to assemble, Mallek-ul-Tija again called a halt, and could scarcely be persuaded by the guide to advance any further, until he earnestly represented that, about a *kōs* further on, they would arrive at a pleasant valley bounded on three sides by mountains, and through which there flowed a broad river of excellent water, while the ground was free from reptiles. Thus urged, again the harassed troops set forward, and about midnight entered the narrow gorge leading to the promised shelter. All was as the guide had foretold; and the toil-worn soldiers, having drunk of the reviving stream, flung themselves down to rest, and were speedily buried in the deep sleep of fatigue.

As soon as they believed themselves unobserved, Sirkeh and the guide hastened to the river's bank,

* An evil spirit of wood and mountain.

and, leaping into a small boat, rowed hastily down the stream. In a few minutes they were out of sight of the spot where their enemies reposed, and in half an hour they had reached the fort of Sirkeh's pretended enemy Sanghir, to whose presence he quickly gained admittance. He informed the Raja, who was, in truth, not only a friend, but a near relation, of all that had befallen him, and explained to him the stratagem by which he had lured the game into his toils. Having concerted a plan of operations, Sanghir immediately despatched messengers to all his commanders, ordering them to send forth their forces in small detached bodies to surround the position of Mallek-ul-Tija. He also sent a fleet courier to the troops of Sirkeh, who, according to their secret instructions, had filed off from the line of march, and now lay encamped at the foot of the hills overlooking the spot occupied by the enemy.

The army of Mallek-ul-Tija remained sunk in deep sleep until a late hour of the morning, and were awoke, every man, by a stranger, who, uttering a war-cry at his side, plunged a dagger into his heart. Thus died the renowned Mallek-ul-Tija and ten thousand of the faithful; and thus was the bloody revenge of the wily Sirkeh fully satiated.

DELHI.

پرده داري ميكند در قصر قيصر عنكبوت
بو مي نوبت ميزند بر كنبد افراسياب

The emperor Shah Jehan, having founded the modern city of Delhi,—still called Shahjehanabad by the Mussulmans,—was desirous of erecting an edifice which should be, at once, a fit habitation for the glorious descendants of the immortal Taimour, and an imperishable memorial of the power and magnificence of the builder. The Badshahi Mahal, the fruit of his design, is still standing—is still the residence of the imperial family; and the boastful inscription surmounting the state presence-chamber, "*If there be a paradise on earth, it is this, it is this, it is this,*" remains as legible as on the day when first engraved. The lofty gates, the spacious courts, and ample halls—the rounded domes, and tapering minarets—the frowning battlements, the jutting towers, the very thrones, stand now as firmly as they stood in the first year of their erection. But,

> Mark how the palace lifts a lying front,
> Concealing, often, in magnific jail,
> Proud want; a deep unanimated gloom!

All the costly beauties of this regal abode are now abandoned to neglect and desolation. Their pride is overrun by grinning poverty; and amid these still solid monuments of former grandeur, a skeleton of royalty remains enshrined. The shadows of departed might and magnificence haunt every avenue,

> The melancholy ghosts of dead renown,
> Whispering faint echoes of the world's applause.

The late emperor, Akbur Shah the Second, was a state prisoner to the British power within the walls of this his own palace, whence he could not move, even for change of air, without permission from the British authorities. He was, however, invariably treated with respect and consideration by his jailers, and although divested of all influence as the monarch of a kingdom, was permitted to exercise despotic authority within the walls of his royal prison, even to the lives of his retainers. He also enjoyed the power of bestowing titles and dresses of honour, subject to the approval of the British government; and, except in a few instances, was not deprived of the control of his own household and family affairs. He was provided with a civil list amply sufficient to save himself and retainers from starvation; and on all occasions of his appearance in public, whether he held a *durbar*, or went to perform religious rites at the Jumma Musjid, or had permission to visit the Kootab Minar for the benefit of his health, this remnant of the most glorious of existing dynasties was attended by a British *guard of honour*.

The personal appearance and bearing of the late emperor was remarkably regal. His features were very regular, his complexion fair, his expression mild and intelligent, his action easy and dignified. The portrait which forms the frontispiece of this volume is an exceedingly faithful likeness; but having been painted by His Glorious Majesty's Portrait-Painter Extraordinary, Alum, it was very properly made to assume the appearance of mid-life rather than of old age. I had the felicity of an interview with the illustrious Great Mogul in the early part of the year 1834, about the time that this portrait was taken. He was then much more aged in appearance than here represented, being seventy-nine years of age, and rendered singularly venerable by his flowing hair and beard, which were bleached to the whiteness of silver. He was greatly respected by all the citizens of Delhi; indeed, his name was reverenced for his descent' sake throughout India, and Mohummedan chiefs from all quarters paid their homage whenever an opportunity offered. He had eight wives, the favourite of whom was dignified with the appellation of Mumtajh Mahal (the honour of the palace), her influence over the monarch being unlimited. His family was large; Mirza Mohummed Aboo Zaffir being the eldest son, and heir-apparent to the *musnud*.

The domestic peace of the emperor was sadly disturbed by the factions of his court; for intrigue appears to have run as high in these days of court famine as in the more plentiful seasons of Akbur the First, or of Shah Jehan. Prince Mirza Sulim, the third son of the emperor, was the royal favourite; and his majesty was for ever scheming, in opposition to the will of the East India Company, to secure the succession in favour of this prince, to the exclusion of Aboo Zaffir; moreover, each of the eight wives had a particular pet to oppose prince Mirza Sulim. Fate, however, removed him from the strife; he died in September 1836, and Aboo Zaffir succeeded his father.

The old emperor was extremely sensitive touching the respect which he deemed due to the dignity of his presence. Lord Amherst was the first British governor-general who visited the court of Delhi, in consequence of the emperor having, until that time, refused to allow even the representative of the British monarch to be seated in the royal presence. It is said that, on the occasion in question, the emperor was so moved by the indignity, that he could not restrain his tears. In 1828, Lord Combermere, as commander-in-chief, paid the emperor a visit, and in addition to the usual honours of the *khilat* and other presents, received the incomprehensible dignities of the Fish and Kettle-drum, with the rank of seven thousand, and the illustrious titles of Ghizenfir-ud-

Dowla, Zaf-ul-Mooluk, Sipahi Sala, Kahn Jehan, Kahn Bahadoor, Roostum Junge; which severally imply—Champion of the State, Sword of the Empire, Commander Supreme, King of the World, Lord and Prince, the Roostum of Battle. The day following his lordship's visit was the anniversary of the emperor's birth, and it happened that a laughable scene occurred, which had like to have terminated in an usurpation of the emperor's *musnud*. The effigies of omras still remaining at court, having assembled in the presence-chamber, were waiting to pay their homage before escorting his majesty to the public thanksgiving at the Jumma Musjid; when a madman, who, though in truth but a humble sweetmeat vendor in the opinion of his fellow-citizens, had for some years lived the life of a monarch within the world of his own mind, gained admittance, and believing himself to be the true Great Mogul, made an attempt to mount the royal throne, just as the emperor entered the *durbar*. The *chobdars* and *hircarras* in attendance succeeded in preventing this desecration of a seat sacred to those who can be styled "Refuge of the Universe;" and seizing the culprit by the hair, began to buffet and cudgel him very unmercifully; but the emperor, being informed that he was insane, graciously ordered the wanderer to be taken care of, and had his castigators severely punished for their cruelty. It is a fact, however, that the same *musnud* was once occupied, with all its concomitant powers and privileges, for the space of six hours, by one of lower degree than this eccentric manufacturer of bulls'-eyes and sugar-stick, to wit, by a common water-carrier.

THE STORY OF KING HUMMAIONE AND THE BIHISTI,

would form the basis of a romance worthy of the Arabian Nights; but being a veritable passage in the history of the Delhi emperors, I will relate it according to the best version, and without embellishment.

In A. D. 1539, the emperor Hummaione, being in personal command of his forces, gave battle to the redoubtable invader Shere Kahn and his Afghan army, upon the banks of the Karamnassur. Hummaione was victorious in the field; but the crafty Afghan succeeded in regaining all the honours and advantages of conquest, and an ample revenge, by a bold stratagem which he carried into effect that same night. While the troops of the emperor were wrapt in sound sleep, and in the fatal security of their previous success, Shere Kahn, with the survivors of his hardy followers, surprised the camp, and massacred thousands of the Moguls. Those who perished not by the sword fled, unarmed, in the confusion of the panic; and the emperor himself would have fallen into the hands of the pursuers, had it not been for the devoted gallantry of three of his chief omras, who nobly sacrificed their lives for his sake, and effected his escape. Trusting to the speed of his faithful charger, Hummaione made for the bridge, but found it destroyed; and, his pursuers being upon his heels, no hope appeared to be left, but to commit himself to the waters. He dashed down the precipitous bank into the torrent, was dismounted in the fall, and carried headlong down the rapid stream; so that his enemies thought that he had perished. His better destiny, however, interposed between him and the abyss of destruction, and he was saved, when almost insensible, by the brave efforts of a *Bihisti*, or water-carrier, who happened to be filling his water-skins at the river-side. Finding himself thus unexpectedly rescued from a watery grave, Hummaione bestowed the rich gift of his royal necklace upon his poor preserver, and promised him, upon his princely faith, that if it should ever please Providence again to restore him to his kingdom, he would, when so requested by the *Bihisti*, place him upon the imperial *musnud*, clothed in the royal robes, and with full liberty to exercise despotic powers as emperor of Hindostan, for the space of six hours.

Not long afterwards Hummaione's good genius was again in the ascendant, and while he was one day employed in transacting the affairs of the state in the royal hall of audience, the *Bihisti* presented himself before the presence, and claimed fulfilment of the emperor's promise. Faithful to his engagement, the generous monarch no sooner recognised his deliverer than he descended from his throne, and causing the *Bihisti* to supply his place, he formally delegated to him authority to exercise all the various functions of the sovereign supreme, himself being the first to perform homage. The *Bihisti* was in no sort abashed by the novelty of his position, or confused by the adulation and officious servility of his courtiers; but, restoring order to the court, he employed his ephemeral authority in framing certain decrees and ordinances in favour of all classes of *Bihistis*, which remain on record (and in force within the palace walls) to this day. The privileges which he thus bestowed on himself and his fellow *Bihistis*, were of the most reasonable and modest kind; and so much was Hummaione pleased with his preserver's conduct, that, on the termination of his short reign, and on the moment of his own re-accession, he elevated the *Bihisti* to permanent rank and distinction as a noble of the realm, and bestowed the solid advantages of comparative wealth and independence upon all the members of his family.

Akbur Shah the Second, died in October, 1837, when nearly eighty-two years of age; he was succeeded by Prince Mirza Mohummed Aboo Zaffir, under the titles of Abool Mozaffir Suruj-ud-Deen Mohummed Bahadoor Sani Shah. In honour of the occasion, royal salutes were fired by the British troops at all the principal military stations, and congratulations, with presents, were forwarded to the new emperor by the governor-general. I have frequently seen this new Great Mogul, and, judging by his appearance, I should say that he cannot be much under sixty years of age, though some allowance be made for the effects of a life of royal excess. His character is not remarkable for anything great or good. The only interesting matter attached to his history is of a very sad nature, and a stain upon his long list of imperial titles. It is thus told :—

Only a few years since, among the attendants of his consort, was a very lovely girl about sixteen years of age, whose charms excited a strong passion in the heart of the prince. Being a virtuous girl, she turned a deaf ear to his entreaties, and rejected all his proffered bribes with scorn; in consequence of which she was put under a severe course of daily punishment, and her delicate person subjected to the most cruel stripes and privation. She bore her sufferings with patient resignation, until they were aggravated beyond human endurance, "when one night, about half-past ten o'clock," according to the account given by the *Durpun*, a native newspaper, "she covered her face with her *chuddur*, and wrapping her *razai* about her, she threw herself from the top of the south-west tower of the palace wall into the dry ditch below, sixty feet; and having broken all her bones, and fractured her skull, the poor child uttered one piercing shriek and expired."

General and particular accounts both of ancient and modern Delhi are to be found in about nine out of every ten Oriental works, whether of history or of personal narrative; I shall, therefore, confine my local descriptions to those scenes which form the immediate subjects of the accompanying plates. Not the city only, but the whole country round about it, would appear to be an inexhaustible mine of antiquarian treasure; and whether the traveller visits it for the first or for the ninety-ninth time, he may find a thousand novelties to delight him, and entice him to a protracted sojourn; if only his love of the truly sublime and beautiful be superior to the extremes of heat, dust, noise, insects, and evil odours. Elves and demons may alike find fitting haunts in Delhi. Among its scattered piles of arched palaces, its pillared courts, out-topped with tapering minarets and shining domes, its heaps of blackened tombs, its prostrate towers, and opening vaults, fantastical romance and brooding mystery, have each their proper homes. Erewhile

> I took it for a fairy region
> Of some gay creatures of the element,
> That in the colours of the rainbow live,
> And play i' th' plighted clouds;

and now, though not a passing shadow has fallen to

Drawn by T. C. Dibdin from a sketch by T. Bacon, Esq.

Ancient Gateway Delhi

change my mood, nor yet a sound has stolen upon the air—

> The tombs
> And monumental caves of death look cold,
> And shoot a chillness to my trembling heart.

Many of the most beautiful specimens of these relics are now dissolving so rapidly, owing to the destructive extremes of the climate, that in a few short years they will be no more seen. The gateway, which is exhibited in the annexed plate, is hastening to the dust. The scorching sun strikes in and opens wide its gaping seams; and the streaming rains of each returning monsoon, as they pour through its crannied walls, are hurrying it, stone by stone, wall by wall, into the ravines below. The style of its architecture is peculiar to the time of Jehanghir, but its history appears to be doubtful; for some among the tradition-vendors at Delhi represent it as having been the entrance to the empress Neur Jehan's state apartments, while others affirm that it formed part of the palace of Etimaun-ud-Dowla, the father of that illustrious lady. Whether it be one or the other, it is equally an object of interest to the natives, who appear to have as much reverence for the name of the father, because he *was* the father of the renowned Neur Jehan, as they have for the memory of the daughter herself. The histories of these celebrated persons are rendered the more imperishable from their connexion with that of the intrepid and persecuted Shere Afghan, who, after having evaded the malice and jealousy of Jehanghir, by a hundred gallant exploits, was at last treacherously murdered by a band of conspirators, acting under the orders of that monarch. Their united histories form one of the most romantic passages in the annals of the Mogul emperors of Delhi. The historian, Tarihk Kahfi Kahn, has related it with but little of those extravagant redundancies which Oriental writers of all ages have esteemed as beauties. It shall, therefore, be told after his version.

THE SUN OF WOMEN; THE LIGHT OF THE HAREM; THE LIGHT OF THE WORLD.

In the reign of the mighty Emperor Akbur,—whose memory still floats upon the tears of the people of all India,—and while the prince Jehanghir was a youth about seventeen years of age, Khaja Aias, a native of western Tartary, quitted his own country in the hope of finding a better fortune in Hindostan. He was descended of an ancient and noble family, now fallen into decay by various revolutions of fortune; though happily his parents were able to bestow upon him an excellent education, worthy of his intelligent mind and goodness of heart. Early in life he fell in love with a very beautiful young woman, as poor as himself; and, in defiance of grinning poverty, they married. Soon after their union, they found it difficult to procure even the bare necessaries of life; and when reduced to the last extremity, Khaja Aias determined upon seeking a change of lot in the western provinces of India, where the army of the Mogul Emperor was an usual resource for all needy Tartars.

All the worldly goods of Khaja Aias consisted of one sorry horse, a well-proved blade, and a very small sum of money, which he had gathered from the sale of his other poor effects. Placing his wife upon the horse, he walked by her side; for she was at that time expecting ere long to present him with their first-born, and could ill endure the fatigue of so arduous a journey. Their scanty pittance of money was very soon exhausted, and they had been reduced to subsist for many days upon the slender gleanings of charity, when they arrived on the borders of the Great Desert, separating Tartary from the dominions of the family of Taimour, in India. No house was there to shelter them from the smiting power of the sun, no hand to relieve their increasing wants. To return was certain misery, destitution, and shame; to proceed, apparent destruction.

They had advanced two or three days' journey into the desert, having kept a long and bitter fast, when, to complete their misfortunes, the poor woman became so ill that she was unable to proceed. She began to reproach her husband for his folly in persuading her, at such a time, to leave her native country, for exchanging a quiet, though poor life, for the ideal prospect of wealth in a foreign country. While they remained in this distressing situation, the poor woman gave birth to a daughter, and they tarried in that place for many hours, vainly hoping that travellers might pass by, from whom they might obtain some relief. But, alas, they were doomed to disappointment. Human feet seldom trod those dreary wastes, and the sun was now declining apace. With the most gloomy forebodings they looked forward to the approach of night, for the place was the haunt of thousands of wild beasts ; and even should Providence enable them to escape death from hunger, they feared that they must fall a prey to the savage monsters of the desert. Khaja Aias, in this sad extremity, having once more placed his wife upon the half-starved horse, found himself so much exhausted that he could with difficulty move his limbs. To carry the child became impossible, and the mother, through excessive weakness, could not even hold herself securely upon her horse. A fearful struggle ensued between humanity and necessity : the latter prevailed, and they at last agreed upon entrusting the child to the care of Providence, by leaving it upon the highway. They placed it upon the ground under the shade of a tree, and covered it with dry leaves ; then taking a tearful farewell of their darling, the disconsolate parents again attempted to proceed.

When they had advanced about a mile from the spot where they had abandoned the infant, the mother being no longer able to discern the tree under which it was laid, gave way to her excessive grief. She cast herself from the horse upon the ground, exclaiming, in heart-rending accents of agony, "My child! my child!" Khaja Aias endeavoured to raise her, but she was unable to support herself, and believing that she was about to die, she cried aloud, and implored that she might be granted a last look at her beloved baby; she rent her hair with despair and remorse for her cruelty in abandoning the infant, while breath remained to her. Khaja Aias was also pierced to the heart with grief at the sight of her anguish, and entreating her to compose herself, he promised to bring her the infant; assuring her that his returning anxiety to recover the child had endowed him with renewed strength. After a painful retrogression he at length regained the spot where they had left the child; but who shall describe the state of mind of that horror-stricken parent when he beheld his first-born enfolded within the deadly coils of a huge serpent! For some minutes his presence of mind was suspended, and his energies were only recalled when he beheld the venomous monster extend its jaws, as if to devour the innocent babe. The bewildered father rushed forward to the rescue, and the serpent, alarmed at his vociferations and the flashing of his sword, retired into the hollow tree, leaving the child uninjured. With a grateful heart he took the infant to his bosom, and returned to his afflicted wife.

He gave it into her arms, and while he was yet relating its miraculous escape, behold, a party of travellers appeared advancing towards them. These proved themselves to be humane persons; for they not only relieved the existing necessities of the sufferers, but furnished them with the means of proceeding comfortably upon their journey. This they did by easy stages, and at length arrived at Lahore, then the capital of the Emperor Akbur.

Here Khaja Aias had the good fortune to meet with a distant relation, by name Asuph, with whom he had formerly been on terms of sworn friendship; and who, being now in high favour with the emperor, hoped to be able to give his newly arrived kinsman some substantial proof of his sincere affection. He first appointed him his own private secretary; and having discovered his great abilities, he himself introduced him at court, where his noble appearance and graceful bearing soon attracted the favourable notice of Akbur. The monarch made immediate inquiries of Asuph concerning him; and having heard his history, and being satisfied of his great abilities and intrepidity, as well as of his firm integrity, he at once raised him to the command of a thousand horse. After a short period of subordinate service, by diligence, rectitude, and temperance, Khaja Aias was raised to the distinguished appointment of steward of the royal household; and again, in process of time, his genius being superior even to his good fortune, he succeeded in advancing himself to the most responsible office in the realm,—the emperor having invested him with the dignity and title of Etimaun-ud-Dowla, High Treasurer of the Empire. Thus, he who had well-nigh perished through want in the desert, became, in the space of a few years, by the excellence of his head and heart, the first and most favoured friend and adviser of the mightiest of earthly monarchs.

The daughter who had been born to Khaja Aias (henceforth to be called Etimaun-ud-Dowla) in the desert, received, by order of the emperor, the title of Mher-ul-Nissa,—the Sun of Women,—and, in truth, she had right good claims to the appellation; for it was already apparent that she would excel all the ladies of the East in beauty. She was educated, as was fit, with the utmost care and attention. In music, in dancing, in poetry, in painting, (for these are the accomplishments of the court ladies,) she had no equal throughout India. Her disposition was lively, her wit acute and discriminate, her spirit lofty and uncontrolled.

When the lovely Mher-ul-Nissa was yet in the first freshness of her beauty, it happened that Sulim, afterwards Jehanghir, then the prince-royal and heir to the throne, visited her father, to witness some sporting entertainment given by that minister. After the amusements had concluded, when the public had withdrawn, and only the principal guests from the palace remained, wine was served, and, according to custom, the ladies were admitted in their veils.

Mher-ul-Nissa was prepossessed by the noble mien of the young prince; and being suddenly fired with a mixed ambition and love, she resolved upon laying siege to his heart; for already had the youthful beauty discovered that, with her, to besiege would, in all likelihood, be to conquer. She sung; the prince was in raptures. She danced; his sense of propriety was scarcely able to restrain him from casting himself immediately at her feet. Her stature,—the glimpses of her shape which from time to time he enjoyed,—her gait and graceful action,—the lovely rotundity of her limbs, as once or twice only he espied them through the silver folds of her ample dress,—all these, mingled with certain whispers of report, had raised his ideas of her beauty to the highest possible pitch; and, at a moment when his eyes appeared as if they would devour her, she, by an affected accident, dropped her veil, and shone upon him, at once, in all the dazzling refulgence of her wonderful beauty. The confusion which she admirably feigned heightened not a little the effect of her charms, and her timorous eye stealthily lighted for a moment upon the prince, and kindled all his soul into a devouring flame of love. He was mute during the rest of the entertainment, and the accomplished Mher-ul-Nissa fixed immoveably, by her wit, the arrow which the unrivalled charms of her person had driven through his heart.

Sulim, distracted by his passion, knew not what course to pursue; for he was well aware that the all-beautiful damsel, the captivator of his heart, had been betrothed by her father to Shere Afghan, a Turkomann nobleman of great renown. In his suspense, he sought the advice of his father Akbur, who, guided by the integrity of his heart, sternly refused to allow any act of injustice to be practised, even in favour of the heir to his throne, his favourite son. The young prince retired from the presence abashed and spirit-broken, and the incomparable Mher-ul-Nissa became the bride of Shere Afghan. This nobleman suffered, however, great prejudice at court from all but the emperor himself, for not having made a voluntary resignation of the lady to the enamoured prince; for, although Sulim dared not to make any open attack upon his fortunate rival during the lifetime of his father, still the courtiers worshipped the rising sun, and threw unmerited contumely and defamation upon Shere Afghan; who, becoming disgusted with his unenviable position, withdrew from the court, and retired to Burdwan, having obtained the government of that district from the Suba of Bengal.

The passion for Mher-ul-Nissa which Sulim had repressed, from respect and fear of his father, returned with accumulated force, when his royal parent died, and he had succeeded to the throne of Delhi. He then became absolute. No subject could thwart his will and pleasure ; and his first act was to recal Shere Afghan from his retreat, with promises of high favour ; for although he had no intention of calling down public opprobrium, by forcibly depriving that chief of his wife, yet he expected to be able quietly to gain his object.

Had Shere Afghan suspected the design of the young monarch, he would inflexibly have refused to obey the mandate of the despot. His heroic strength and bravery had rendered him extremely popular among the soldiery. He was naturally high-spirited and proud ; and it was not to be expected that he would tamely yield to indignity and public shame. His prowess and his courage were equalled only by his good fortune, so that his personal reputation was already very high. Born of noble parents in Turkomania, he had spent his youth in Persia, having served with uncommon renown under Shah Ishmael the Third. His original name was Asta Jilho ; but having slain a lion single-handed, he was dignified with the title of Shere Afghan, signifying the overthrower of lions. Under the latter name he had become both famous and popular throughout India, and in the wars of Akbur had served with great distinction. He had reaped a profusion of laurels under Kahn Kahnan, at the taking of Sihnd, by exhibiting prodigies of strength and valour. Preferments had been heaped upon him by Akbur, who loved to behold in others that daring intrepidity for which he was himself remarkable. Jehanghir held his court at Delhi at the time when he called Shere Afghan to his presence. The doughty chief answered the royal summons in person, and was not only very graciously received with words of welcome, but was loaded with new honours; for being naturally open and generous, he suspected not the emperor's treacherous intentions. Time, thought he, has erased from the mind of Jehanghir all recollections of Mher-ul-Nissa. Alas! how soon was his confidence abused!

The monarch, being impatient for the accomplishment of his wishes, determined upon removing his rival from his path, without loss of time; and the means to which he had recourse were at once foolish and disgraceful. He appointed a day for a great hunting expedition, and gave orders to his couriers and *shikarris* that they should endeavour to discover the haunts of all the most formidable tigers which were to be found in the jungul. News was quickly brought to him that a tiger of a very extraordinary size and of terrible ferocity, which had been for many days committing fearful havoc and devastation in the villages, and had hitherto destroyed all the *shikarris* who had arrayed themselves against him, now lay concealed in the forest of Nidarbhari. So monstrous and powerful a brute was this tiger that he was said to have carried away, upon his back, many of the largest oxen and buffaloes from the neighbouring herds. Jehanghir, accompanied by three or four hundred of his chiefs and nobles, and all their several trains, went immediately in pursuit of this savage monster. Having, according to the custom of the Moguls, surrounded the creature's retreat for many miles, they began to move on all sides towards the centre. The tiger was soon roused; and his roaring being heard in all quarters, the emperor ordered his elephant to be driven to the spot.

The nobility being assembled on all sides, Jehanghir called aloud and said, "Who among you will advance, single-handed, and attack this tiger?" At first they stared in mute amazement, wondering if their ears had deceived them; but when the emperor repeated his question, every eye was turned upon Shere Afghan. He appeared not to understand their meaning, conceiving that the emperor was speaking in jest, and never supposing that any one would rashly enter upon so foolish and dangerous an exploit. At length, however, three chiefs, sacrificing their fears to shame, made their salaams to the prince, and each begged permission to try his prowess in single combat, upon the formidable brute. The pride of Shere Afghan was aroused. The three nobles, having offered themselves for the enterprise, were now bound in honour to insist upon their priority; and being afraid of losing his former renown, he thus addressed the three champions, in presence of the emperor. "To attack a poor defenceless animal with weapons, although single-handed, is both unmanly and unfair. God has given to man, no less than to tigers, limbs and sinews; and he has added reason to the former, in order that he may wisely employ his strength." The three chiefs objected, in vain, that all men were inferior to tigers in strength, and that therefore they must be given the aid of steel. "I will convince you of your mistake," replied the hero; and throwing down his sword and shield, he dismounted his elephant, and advanced, unarmed, to meet the enraged tiger.

Though the emperor was in secret pleased with a proposal so much in accordance with his barbarous design, he made a show of dissuading him from the trial. Shere Afghan's spirit of adventure, however, was excited, and he determined to enter upon the struggle. The monarch, feigning reluctance, at last yielded, and gave permission for him to advance. The assembled chiefs knew not whether they ought most to admire the courage of the man, or to exclaim against the folly of the deed. Astonishment was painted in every face. Every tongue was silent. Various writers have given minute but incredible details of the encounter. Thus much however is certain, that after a long and desperate fight, the wonderful warrior prevailed, and though horribly bruised and lacerated, he at last laid the monster dead at his feet. So miraculous did the victory appear, that historians have said that the eye-witnesses of the action were almost afraid to vouch for its truth, although the facts could be proved by the concurrent testimony of thousands. The fame of Shere Afghan increased, and was spread abroad through all Asia. The evil designs of the emperor had hitherto failed, but they stopped not here; his determined cruelty, and the impatience of his passion, suggested and urged him to the employment of other treacherous expedients against the life of the persecuted hero.

Shere Afghan had scarcely recovered from his wounds when he came to pay his respects at court. He was caressed by the emperor, and in the candour of his own heart he suspected not the treachery of his master. Meanwhile a new snare, and one more likely to prove fatal, was prepared for him. Jehanghir basely gave orders to one of his elephant drivers to waylay the chief, in one of the narrow streets leading to the palace; and, when he should next pass that way, to make a feint, as though his elephant were ungovernable, and cause him to tread the invincible warrior to death; hoping that he might escape suspicion, as accidents of that nature are not unfrequent, owing to the indomitable rage of those animals at certain seasons. It happened

Drawn by I. C. Dibdin from a Sketch by I. Bacon, Esqr

Engraved by Capone

Baoli, and remains of Jehanghir's Palace, Delhi.

London. Published Oct. 1, 1839 for the Proprietor by Charles Tilt, 86 Fleet Street

that the next time Shere Afghan passed that way he rode in his palanquin; and, seeing the infuriated elephant in his way, he gave orders to his bearers to turn back, fearing that some of them might suffer. The elephant, however, charged upon them before they could make their escape, and the chief's cowardly crew of slaves dropped his palanquin under the animal's feet, and fled. Shere Afghan saw his imminent peril just in time to rise. Springing boldly to his feet, he drew a short sword, which he always carried at his side; and, making a furious attack upon the elephant, he struck across the root of the trunk, and with one blow, severed it from the head. The poor animal roared with anguish, and, turning from his opponent, fled, until, from the copious loss of blood which ensued, he fell and expired.

The emperor, who had been watching the success of his plan, from a window on the east side of the palace, retired from the scene in amazement and shame; yet was his duplicity so great that he received the chief without emotion, and listened to his relation of the adventure with well-feigned astonishment. He loudly applauded his bravery and prowess, so that Shere Afghan departed from the presence, well-pleased and unsuspicious. But although the crafty monarch covered the villany of his heart with a smooth face, the fire of his vengeance was not extinguished, but rather burned the more fiercely; and

F

being now convinced of the necessity of acting with greater forethought, he suffered his rival to retire again into Bengal, in order that he might the more surely arrange a plot for his destruction. He was led to adopt this measure, since he could not but be convinced that he had now betrayed his infamous designs to many of his courtiers: among whom, indeed, his foul practices, so disgraceful to the character of a great prince, had become a common theme of gossip, and the mark of their secret vituperations.

Despotic monarchs, however, are never without courtiers who flatter their worst passions, and pander to their most pernicious pleasures. Nor was the court of Jehanghir an exception to this trite remark; for, had there been in the presence no other sycophant, Kootab, Suba of Bengal, was in himself a host. This heartless villain, in order that he might ingratiate himself with his royal master—for it has never been proved that he acted by the king's express commands—hired a band of forty desperadoes, to whom he entrusted the formidable task of attacking and murdering Shere Afghan, as soon as an opportunity should present itself. The friends of the hero, however, found means to apprise him of this nefarious scheme, and he in consequence determined upon remaining within his doors, until he should be able to discern from what quarter the blow would be aimed; although such was his confidence in his own strength and valour, that he would not suffer any alteration in the usual habits of his household. He would not permit his followers to remain in his house during the night, because he knew it to be their custom to depart each man to his own house after he had retired to rest. An aged porter was the only domestic who remained under his roof; and of this circumstance, which indeed is common throughout India, the assassins were not ignorant. They made a careful examination of the premises, and found that on the right-hand side, immediately within the entrance, there was a room, used by the chief as a writing-chamber, communicating with his sleeping apartment by a narrow passage. This they determined to make their rendezvous, and accordingly, after dark, they took advantage of the temporary absence of the old porter, and conveyed themselves without discovery into the house.

At night, the principal entrance having been closed according to custom, Shere Afghan and his family retired to rest at the usual hour. Some of the assassins, when they thought it probable that he had fallen asleep, stole noiselessly into his apartment, and prepared to plunge their daggers into his body. But one of them, who was an old man, being touched with remorse, cried out with a loud voice, "Hold! hold! my brethren; have we not the Suba's orders for what we do? Let us then behave like men, and do our duty with humanity, though firmly.

Shall forty fall upon one, and that one asleep?" "Boldly spoken, my friend," replied the awakened Shere Afghan, starting from his bed, and seizing his sword; "and shall one brave man, from whose right hand thousands, aye, thousands of gallant warriors, and much more terrible antagonists, have drunk the black waters of death, tamely submit to be butchered by a handful of cowards! Down, down, ye craven-hearted villains!" and with determined intrepidity the hero rushed upon his foes. Death was dealt by almost every blow from his mighty arm; and, in a few minutes, more than one half of the traitors were weltering in their blood. Only four or five, indeed, survived; and they were so severely wounded that they were unable to make their escape. The old man who had given the alarm did not attempt to fly, and Shere Afghan, taking him kindly by the hand, praised his conduct, and thanked him for that compassionate intervention, without which he would doubtless have been sacrificed. He then inquired particularly of him concerning those under whose orders the assassins had acted, and, having been fully informed, he dismissed him with handsome presents, telling him to make all the particulars as public as possible.

The fame of this gallant exploit resounded throughout the whole empire, and Shere Afghan could with difficulty move abroad, in consequence of the dense crowd of persons, who pressed around him on all sides with congratulations and applause. He, however, thought it wise to retire from the capital of Bengal to his old residence at Burdwan, hoping to live there in obscurity and peace with his beloved Mher-ul-Nissa. He was deceived. Kootab had received his appointment as Suba of Bengal, upon the express condition that he should find some effectual and speedy method of destroying this heroic chieftain, and he set diligently to work for the performance of his obligation. After deliberating upon the best means to be employed, he at last devised a scheme which unhappily enabled him to accomplish his murderous purpose. He resolved upon making a tour through the provinces under his government; and having settled his affairs at Tanda, which was then the capital of Bengal, he immediately set forth in state, accompanied with a large retinue. In his route he visited Burdwan, and made it no secret among his officers that he had the emperor's orders to despatch Shere Afghan. That renowned warrior, ever resolved upon performing his duties in defiance of all danger, no sooner heard of the Suba's arrival, than he mounted his charger, and, with only two attendants, went forth to pay his respects to the representative of his sovereign. The treacherous Suba received him with profound respect and politeness. They rode for some time side by side, and their conversation turned upon indifferent affairs, until they approached the walls of the city, when the Suba halted, and mounted his elephant of state, under pretence of appearing with becoming pomp before the inhabitants of Burdwan. Shere Afghan reined up his horse while the Suba was ascending the *haoda*, and at this moment one of the pikemen, pretending that the chief was in the way of his master, struck his horse with his weapon, and began to drive it before him. Shere Afghan, enraged at the insult, and knowing that the slave would not have ventured upon such an abominable insolence without his master's orders, perceived that a new plot was laid against his life. He turned suddenly upon the pikeman, and threatened him with instant death, whereupon that cowardly wretch fell to the ground, and cried that he was slain. Swords were immediately drawn. Shere Afghan had no time to deliberate. He spurred his gallant charger up to the royal elephant, and tearing down the *haoda*, at one blow clove the skull of the recreant Suba in twain, from the crown to the chin. Then turning his reeking sword upon the attendant nobles, he first of all slew the Suba's counsellor and confidential friend, Aba Kahn, an Omra of five thousand horse, and each successive blow laid prostrate in the dust another chief. Panic-struck at the deadly powers of the renowned hero, the whole body of nobles fled with their attendants to a distance; and Shere Afghan, believing that he had effectually rid himself of his enemies, began to look to the state of his wounds. When his dastardly foes saw this, they checked their flight, and, rallying upon an eminence at a short distance, began to fire upon their brave opponent with bows and match-locks. The proud and heroic chief disdained to fly; and, as the missiles fell thickly about him, he bitterly upbraided the soldiers with their cowardice, and challenged each of the chiefs to combat; but he spoke in vain, for they continued their murderous fire, and he received many wounds from each successive discharge. In his extremity, when about to renew his attack, a ball struck his horse in the forehead, and killed it on the spot. Then, beholding the shadow of death upon the book of his destiny, the noble Shere Afghan turned his face towards Mecca, and taking a handful of dust for want of water, poured it upon his head. With perfect composure he repeated his last prayer, and while his lips yet moved, several balls entered his breast, and he fell lifeless before his dastardly enemies, who even then were afraid to approach him, until satisfied that life was quite extinct.

When the arrow of death is shot from the bow of fate,
The shield of circumspection will be thoroughly pierced.

No sooner was it ascertained that he was in truth dead than one of the officers hastened to the residence of the slain Shere Afghan, for the purpose of conveying the tidings to Mher-ul-Nissa, fearing that if it were incautiously communicated to her, she might, in the first paroxysms of her grief, destroy herself. That lady, however, bore her misfortune with more fortitude and resignation than could have been expected; and in answer to the pressing overtures of Jehanghir, she declared her intention of following the injunctions of her deceased lord, who, she alleged, had clearly foreseen his ultimate destruction, through the emperor's passion, and had frequently conjured her, when so solicited, to yield implicit obedience to the royal will. She was therefore sent with all imaginable care to Delhi; and, as she recalled to mind the tenderness with which the young prince Sulim had regarded her in former days, she was fully reconciled to her fate, and looked forward with delight to the glorious prospect of becoming the favourite sultana of the most powerful monarch in the world. Her vanity, however, was doomed to present disappointment; for although she was received with great affection and respect by Rohkia Sultana, the emperor's mother, the mind of that prince appeared to be strangely altered, for he resolutely declined receiving her, and would not even grant her an interview. Whether remorse had entered his soul, or whether his attention was then engaged by a new object, is uncertain. All authors, however, agree, that he was so much afflicted at the death of his favourite, the Suba of Bengal, that he determined upon punishing Mher-ul-Nissa for an offence in which she had taken no part. Whatever the true motive might have been, certain it is that he sternly ordered her to be confined in one of the inferior apartments of the seraglio, a large dilapidated chamber, which had remained many years desolate and uninhabited. Contrary to his usual munificence to women, he also restricted her to a miserable allowance of fourteen *annas*, something less than two shillings of English money daily, for the subsistence of herself and her slaves.

Mher-ul-Nissa was a woman of a haughty spirit, and could ill brook such contumelious treatment; yet for a long time she found no remedy, and gave herself up to grief and despair. At length, her spirit recovered its natural elasticity, and hope came to console her in her affliction—hope that she might yet find an opportunity of re-kindling the emperor's passion. She was confident in the power of her amazing beauty, if she could only bring it to bear upon the monarch; but although Rohkia Sultana, who was deeply interested in her fate, used all her eloquence in her favour, she could not prevail upon her son to alter his conduct, or in any measure to relax his extraordinary enmity towards the beautiful widow. The ready invention of Mher-ul-Nissa, however, set her upon various schemes for bringing about what she so ardently desired; and for the purpose of raising her reputation in the seraglio, and of supporting herself and slaves in something more like comfort, she began to employ her taste and invention in the cultivation of poetry and other elegant arts, and also in working some admirable pieces of tapestry and embroidery, in painting silks with exquisite delicacy, and in many other equally lady-like and profitable accomplishments. The fruits of her labour and ingenuity were sold by her slaves among the more opulent ladies, in the squares of the royal seraglio, and in the harems of the nobles; and being elegant beyond anything of the kind which had been before seen, and possessing additional interest from the history of the fair artist who wrought them, were bought with the greatest avidity, and at the most extravagant prices. Nothing was fashionable among the great ladies of Delhi and Agra but the work of her hands; and by the traffic of her pretty wares she soon accumulated so large a sum of money, that she was enabled to repair and beautify her apartment, and to clothe her slaves in the richest tissues and brocades; while she herself affected a very plain and simple dress, without any sort of ornament.

In this situation the beautiful widow of Shere Afghan continued during four years, without having once seen the emperor. Her fame reached his ears from all quarters, and he at length found his resolution giving way to curiosity. He resolved upon surprising her, and therefore, communicating his design to no one, he suddenly entered her apartments. He found everything so elegant and costly where he had expected to behold the miserable and poverty-stricken walls of a prison, that he was struck with amazement and unexpected admiration. Superb and tasteful as was everything around, yet by far the most incomparable ornament of the place was the beauty herself; so that it was some little time ere Jehanghir noticed that, while she herself was clothed in plain white muslin, her slaves who sat around her were glittering in the most rich and dazzling costumes, loaded with jewels. Mher-ul-Nissa, nothing astonished by this sudden visit, slowly arose from her recumbent posture, and, with a well-feigned confusion, saluted the emperor with the customary salaam, touching first the ground and then her forehead with her right hand. She did not utter a word, but stood with her deeply-shrouded eyes fixed upon the emperor's embroidered slippers. Jehanghir, too, remained for many moments silent, overcome by her extraordinary beauty and that inexpressible voluptuousness of mien which it is quite impossible to disregard. At length, having in a measure recovered from his embarrassment, he seated himself upon the low couch which Mher-ul-Nissa had occupied when he had entered, and requested in the most respectful terms that she would condescend to sit by his side.

"Ravisher of hearts," said Jehanghir, "I pray thee be pleased to explain to me what is meant by this strange distinction which I behold in the habits of the illustrious Mher-ul-Nissa and that of her lowly attendants? The former so poor and plain, and the latter so costly!"

"Those born to servitude, most potent monarch, lord of the universe, favourite of Heaven," replied the beauty, with an air of deep submission yet of arch reproach, "must always be clad as it shall please them whom they serve. These young women are my servants, and I seek to alleviate the burden of my bondage by the exercise of my charity; it is indeed my wish to allow them every indulgence which it is in my power to afford. But I myself, being the slave of another, am bound to observe my lord's will and pleasure, even in a small matter. For this reason it is that your majesty finds me habited like a miserable captive."

Although the emperor could not but perceive in this speech the cutting sarcasm which it was intended to convey, the spirited rebuke which it aimed at him for his own unreasonable behaviour, still it was so pertinent, so well turned, that it immediately won his favour no less than his admiration, and he felt all his former affection welling forth from the recesses of his heart with renewed force. Embracing her with great warmth, though respectfully, he declared his love; and, fixing the next day for his nuptials, he issued orders for a public festival to be held in all parts of his dominions.

The ceremony was performed with the most extravagant pomp, and the name of Mher-ul-Nissa was cast aside for that of Neur-Mahal, Light of the Harem. From that day forth all other favourites vanished from before her; and, during the remainder of Jehanghir's reign, she bore the chief sway in all the affairs of the empire.

The wonderful influence of Neur-Mahal was first evinced in the immediate advancement of her family. Her father, Etimaun-ud-Dowla, formerly Khaja Aias, who had been high-treasurer in the reign of Akbur, was now raised to the office of absolute vizier of the empire. Her two brothers were made nobles of the highest rank; and all her numerous relations, who poured into the court from Tartary, upon hearing of the good-fortune of their kinswoman, were advanced to offices of honour and emolument. All whose cause she espoused were sure of promotion. According to her pleasure, they were provided with present power and wealth, or the means of attaining rank and influence by their abilities and exertions. Her father became a great and excellent minister, and his name is highly revered at this day. When, after several years of talented and successful administration of the affairs of the state, he was gathered to his fathers A. D. 1618, he was interred at Agra, and his daughter raised a splendid mausoleum in honourable commemoration of his many virtues. The historian Abul Fazil relates of her, as a proof of her great affection for her father, that in order worthily to perpetuate his memory, she had given orders to erect a monument of solid silver over his remains; but the imperial architect shrewdly remarked, that so precious a material would in all probability be the least enduring of all, as a means of transmitting the vizier's fame to posterity.—"All ages," said he, "are full of avarice; and even the empire of the house of Taimour, like all things mundane, will be subject to revolution and change." She altered her purpose, and built a magnificent fabric of stone at Agra, which remains to this day, and appears likely to transmit to many generations yet to come the illustrious name of Etimaun-ud-Dowla.

The name Neur-Mahal, which had been recently bestowed on Mher-ul-Nissa, was afterwards changed to Neur-Jehan, Light of the World; and in distinction from the other Sultanas, she was styled Shahi, Empress. Her talents were equal even to her beauty; and by her influence over Jehanghir, she became, to all intents and purposes, absolute sovereign of the empire during his life. She survived him about twenty years, and died in A. D. 1646, having spent her second widowhood in retirement and study. That far-famed work of art, the Tajh Mahal, at Agra, was erected to her memory by Shah Jehan, the son and successor of Jehanghir.

ELICHPOOR AND MUNGROOL.

If the bow of difficulty be strung with faith,
It will not fail to propel miracles.

MENU.

THE names attached to localities in the East generally have their origin in some circumstance connected with the history or quality of the country. Elichpoor, or, as the natives properly call it, Elachipoor, signifies the place of cardamoms; and the traveller who intends making it his resting-place, will possibly be disposed to think comfortable things concerning fragrant spice-gardens or nicely-seasoned viands, and may be apt to indulge in other pleasant anticipations of this well-titled city; until he is informed that it lies immediately between two rivers called the Sampun (the stream of snakes), and the Bichun (the stream of scorpions). I am not aware that these deadly reptiles are unusually abundant in the surrounding country; but certainly the very names of its waters might deter a nervous man from pitching his tents in the neighbourhood.

Elichpoor is a considerable city, and the capital of

the province of Berar. Its fortifications are extensive, but weak, being badly planned and badly built, although capable of being made very impracticable to an enemy, owing to the natural difficulties of the position. The place is of great antiquity, and has been the scene of a thousand reverses; especially in its early resistance to the Mohummedan power, having been continually subdued, and continually in revolt. In A.D. 1294, when governed by Elloo Raja, a tributary of the Hindoo sovereigns of Dowlutabad, it made a truly gallant defence, and held out to the utmost extremity of endurance against the conquering arms of Alla-ud-Deen. Since that time, its vicissitudes of fortune have been very extraordinary, and too numerous to be recounted. At last it became, as it still remains, dependent upon the Nizam of the Dekkan.

The group of buildings forming the subject of the annexed engraving are situated on the north side of the city, at no great distance from the gate. They are built upon the bank of a small stream which has its source in the neighbouring mountains, and which, after a tortuous course of only a few miles, passes through the cantonment and falls into the river Sampun, upon the south side of the city. Raiman Shah Doola, whose tomb is the most conspicuous building in the picture, was a fighting priest, half soldier, half saint, a most valiant commander and an undoubted worker of miracles; at once, as he himself boasted,

Drawn by W. Warren, from a sketch by Capt.ⁿ Meadows Taylor. Engraved by S. Fisher.

Shrine of Raiman Shah Doola Elichpoor.

London Published Oct. 1. 1839. by Charles Tilt, 86 Fleet Street.

Alexander and Mohummed. The natives, in pointing out the tomb of this extraordinary personage, never fail to relate the following legend which is attached to it, and concerning which, without doubt, they religiously believe every particular.

THE HEADLESS HERO.

The religious and warlike enthusiasm of Raiman Shah Doola, no less than his followers' love of plunder, induced him to co-operate with Alla-ud-Deen in his invasion of these provinces. But valorous as was Alla-ud-Deen, and impetuous as were his troops, the valour of the one and the impetuosity of the other were contemptible, when compared with the enthusiastic heroism and blood-thirsty passion of Raiman Shah Doola and his devoted followers. Unable to command the ebullitions of their warlike and religious fervour, these death-dispensing preachers pricked on ahead of the main army, converting or slaughtering all the Hindoo inhabitants of the country.

They were of course too daring to think of circumspection, so it happened that at Baitool they unexpectedly encountered the entire force of the Hindoo army. It is said that on the first attack, by their extraordinary valour, they speedily put the pagans to the rout, despite the heroic efforts of their commander, who was himself a soldier of wonderful prowess, strength, and courage. They then pursued them through the rocky mountain passes in the direction of Elichpoor, a countless host of the benighted flying before a little handful of the faithful. Yet no sooner did the routed Hindoos fairly behold the extraordinary disproportion between the two forces, than recovering from their panic, they once more rallied, and offered an effectual resistance to their pursuers. Hereupon, again taking heart, they hotly attacked the enemy in their turn, and hemming them in on all sides, commenced an exterminating and merciless slaughter. Perplexed by the intersecting defiles, ravines, and complicated passes, by which they were surrounded, the little band of Mohummedans knew they could never make good a retreat, and their only alternative was to endeavour to advance by cutting a way through their swarming opponents.

Raiman Shah Doola was in himself a host, and thousands of the infidels fell beneath his mighty arm; until, at last, the two commanders chanced to meet face to face. They paused; and, letting fall their weapons' points upon the earth, surveyed each his foe from head to foot, and appeared to regard each other with looks of disappointment and surprise, mixed with contempt. "That such a one as this," thought either chief, "should dare to stand in my path! What is he more than many vaunting champions who have been reduced to drink of the cold waters of death at my hand?" Thus the heroes paused; and, as it were with mutual consent, stepped back a pace or two, again to scan the figure of his antagonist. The reeking blade of each was purple to the hilt, his bare limbs painted high with gore, his armour dyed in the ruddy life-stream of a thousand victims. But soon the curled lip and bitter glance of scorn chased from their minds all thoughts but those of kindling enmity and strife; and as the thunder clouds of defiance gathered upon their darkling brows, the adverse warriors, in sullen silence, raised on high their shields; and each, grasping again with impassioned grip his thirsty sword, hurled a venomed curse through his clenched teeth, and rushed with deadly fury to the encounter. Shock followed shock, and each repelled attack was answered by another, till their clashing arms and loud-resounding blows were heard loud above the din of the surrounding battle. Then the warring multitudes ceased their strife, and stood around in mixed array to gaze upon the contest of their leaders.

> Three times they breathed, and three times did they drink,
> Upon agreement;

for their struggle lasted from the rising till the setting of the sun. That burning luminary had just dipped upon the horizon when the godlike Raiman Shah Doola cast a furtive glance of regret at its departing glory; and, being for a moment blinded by its slanting rays, his devoted head was instantly struck from his shoulders by his more wary adversary. It appears that this blow, which would have quenched the spirit of all ordinary combatants, did not in the present instance put an immediate end to the fight; for all authentic histories of that time affirm that the engagement between the commanders was hotly kept up until midnight, and the headless chief continued to struggle on with unabated courage, although his blows were dealt with less effect than heretofore; and step by step he was compelled to retreat. At last, fainting from loss of blood, his weapon became useless in his hand, and he fell lifeless to the earth, in a vain attempt to reach the stream of water which may be seen in the accompanying drawing.

Some historians relate that this wonderful hero carried his head under his arm during his retreat, carefully protecting it with his shield against further injury. By others it is affirmed that the still sensible head rolled beside its valorous owner, encouraging him to the contest, by uttering loud unearthly shouts of applause upon all his efforts, and hoarse curses against his enemy. A third account maintains that the head followed and rejoined the trunk on the return of day, fearing that it might be confounded with the pusillanimous thousands which covered the field of battle. Whichever be the true version of the legend, all agree that the body of this sanctified warrior was in the morning found complete where his mangled trunk had fallen; and the faithful assure the visitor that many miracles which were wrought by his bloodless corse gave evidence that he was under the especial favour of Alla and the Prophet. His remains were interred with all the pomp and distinction due to their extraordinary merits, and the mausoleum which bears his name was raised over them.

Since the day of his death the fame of Raiman Shah Doola has continued to spread throughout the Dekkan, and his tomb is the resort of pilgrims from the most distant provinces. Is a mother childless, a father wifeless, a poor man friendless, a rich man sore at heart or afflicted with disease; does a farmer desire to avert blight or secure propitious weather; would the herdsman see his flocks increased a hundred-fold; has the dying man a desire to live, he who is weary of life a wish to die, or the happy and contented person a disposition to be thankful? let him hasten to the shrine of Raiman Shah Doola; especially upon the glorious anniversary of his death. The Moollas declare, and we may readily believe that, out of the thousands, the millions, who perform the pilgrimage, very many have their reward, crowds indeed obtain what they seek; and it is very correctly affirmed by the faithful, that those who are suffered to depart disappointed have failed only because they have not succeeded in rendering themselves acceptable to the saint. The more favoured of the devotees have testified their gratitude for the miraculous favour of the saint, by erecting, one a mosque, another a *serai*, a third a *ghât*, a fourth a gateway, a fifth a cemetery; some have built tombs in honour of the most renowned of Raiman Shah Doola's followers, and others have testified the same respect for subsequent saints or heroes. The scene is one peculiarly adapted to the gay and picturesque processions which so frequently take place there, and is the spot selected for the imposing ceremonies of the Mohurrum festival.

There are several public buildings worthy of notice in and around Elichpoor, beside those here exhibited. The most interesting are the Houz Kutora, the Eedghur, and the tomb of Moni Joni. The Houz Kutora is upon the westward side of the city, surrounded by a magnificent grove of mango trees. It is erected in the centre of a circular reservoir of water, and consists of three octagonal stories, each surrounded by an arched viranda. It is still an imposing building, though clipped of its fair proportions by the ruthless hand of Ishmael Kahn Punni, the grandfather of the present Nawab, who appropriated the materials for building part of the city wall. Above its present roof there were formerly two other stories, in the same style of architecture, surmounted with a beautiful dome of white marble. It is said to have been erected by Moni Joni, a nauchni, or dancing-girl, of unrivalled beauty and fascination, who lived at the court of one of the kings of Gawilghur, and whose charms gained her the privilege of a key to the royal treasury. Little, however, is known of Moni Joni's history, or of the dark times in which she lived: her name has been conveyed to the ears of the present generation by the tomb which bears her name, and which possibly owes its long preservation to its propinquity to that of the presiding saint, above-mentioned.

All the Dekkan provinces, from time immemorial, have been notorious for their hordes of rapacious and sanguinary banditti; and more especially the mountainous districts east and west of Elichpoor, as far as Surat on one side, and Nagpoor on the other. The extirpation of them by Sultan Mohummed Shah, about the middle of the fourteenth century, is a terrible instance of despotic justice. It is thus related by Ferishta. "The banditti of the Dekkan, famous through all countries for their daring robberies on caravans, he determined to root out entirely. For this purpose he issued his royal mandate to the governors of all the provinces, commanding them that they should use their utmost diligence in clearing their countries of thieves and plunderers, by putting them to death without mercy, and that they should send the heads of the victims to the capital, to prove their rigid execution of his orders. Such expedition was employed in this matter, that, in six or seven months, there remained not a sign of these offenders in the kingdom. Nearly eight thousand heads were brought to Koolboorga from different parts, and were piled up in heaps near the city, as examples of the royal justice."

Unfortunately these terrible warnings no longer exist, which circumstance may possibly account for the audacity of the Dekkan marauders of the present day; for certain it is that the whole province, and more especially the northern borders, with Elichpoor and the mountainous country round about it, are thickly infested with hordes of *dukhaits*, *thugs*, and other murderous desperadoes; and although Europeans may travel with comparative safety, it is not so even with the highest and wealthiest classes of the natives. It is only lately that the diabolical system of *thuggi* has been fully exposed, and now vigorous measures have been adopted by the British government for its complete suppression. The confessions of some of the perpetrators who have been brought to justice, are almost too appalling to be credited. I subjoin the following facts, which I have taken from Captain Sleeman's report of a case that occurred at Elichpoor; they form a fair specimen of the system, though by no means so horror-fraught as some others which have transpired. The deponent was a celebrated *thug*, named Sheik Inaent: his confession is freely translated:—

"It was on my return from the first expedition which I made with my father to the Dekkan, when

I was fifteen years of age, and about thirty-five years since, that I was first present at the accomplishment of *thuggi*. We formed a gang of about eighty or ninety *thugs*, under the command of my father Hinga; and it happened that some chiefs of the Dekkan, travelling through Elichpoor, quartered themselves in the mausoleum of Raiman Shah Doola. Two of our scouts, named Gungoo and Laljoo, were strolling through the bazaar for the purpose of collecting information of travellers or others who might be worthy to become our victims, when they fell in with the grooms of the Nawab Subzi Kahn, the uncle of the Nawab Huzeer Mohummed Kahn, of Bhopal. Having entered into conversation with these men, our scouts learnt that the Nawab had been, with his son and a body of two hundred horse, in the service of the Nizam at Hyderabad, but having quarrelled with his son, he had withdrawn from his command, and was returning home to Bhopal. With this information Gumboo and Laljoo returned to our chiefs, and it was agreed that Duleel and Khuleel, two of our leaders, who were the most famous for their exploits, and who possessed the greatest address, should make an excuse for introducing themselves to the Nawab, and gain his confidence. This they did, representing that they had been into the Dekkan with horses for sale, and were now returning to the upper provinces, laden with the fruits of their traffic, and then suggesting that it would be to both parties a mutual advantage and protection, if the Nawab would permit them to join him on the march. Subzi Kahn was much pleased with their manners and appearance, and invited them to join him the next day, when they would set forward.

"Subzi Kahn was attended by two grooms, two troopers, and a slave girl whose duty it was to prepare his *subzi*, or *bhang* (an intoxicating drug), which he was accustomed to take in such large quantities, as to have acquired the name by which he was now universally known. He had considerable property with him, besides three horses and a pony. Our leaders joined him with as many of our gang as it was thought safe to exhibit; others were sent forward as spies upon the road.

"We marched together three stages upon the best possible terms; and on the fourth day's march, about sunrise, we entered an extensive jungul on the hither side of Dhoba, in the district of Baitool. The march was continued until about nine o'clock, when we arrived upon the bank of a small stream. Khuleel, who had been in merry conversation with the Nawab, then said, 'Kahn Sahib, we have had a fatiguing journey; had we not better rest here for a short time, and take a little refreshment?' 'By all means,' said the Nawab; 'I, too, feel a little weary, and shall be glad of my *subzi*.'

"Subzi Kahn then dismounted, laid his sword and shield upon the ground, spread his carpet, and sat down, inviting Duleel and Khuleel to be seated beside him, while the slave girl prepared his *subzi*. Laljoo also, as one of good birth, seated himself near the Nawab, and Gomani stood behind him, appearing to be much interested in the conversation. It was necessary for the *thugs* to have this strong party placed around the Nawab, for he was a very bold and powerful man, and would probably have made but too good use of a moment's warning. The grooms were at this time engaged with the horses, and the troopers were smoking their pipes at a distance, listening to some jocular tale from a facetious fellow of our party, while death stood at their elbows. All things being prepared, and the coast clear, the Nawab was suddenly strangled by Gomani, while Laljoo and Duleel held his legs. In the same instant his followers were likewise despatched; and in less than ten minutes from the time when the Nawab and his followers were all laughing and chatting, their lifeless forms were buried beneath large stones in the bed of the water-course.

Our booty consisted of a gold bracelet, twenty-five gold coins, and fifty rupees, some valuable arms and weapons, cloths, and a very handsome bird-cage, besides the horses and pony. The distribution of the booty was thus made; Khuleel received the most valuable horse, my father had another, Duleel and Gungoo the third, and Gomani and Laljoo the pony, which was a very handsome one. We are always very cautious in disposing of our plunder. Khuleel sent his horse home for his own use, my father sold his at Boorhanpoor, Duleel parted with his at Omraöti, and Gomani kept the pony for many years. Gomani had, however, nearly brought us into difficulty by his imprudence; for, having received in his share a very handsome shield, he carried it to the bazaar in Elichpoor, and offered it for sale, at the ridiculous price of eight rupees; in consequence of which folly, on his part, suspicion was excited, and the people could not help remarking that it was sold too cheaply to have been honestly obtained. Gomani hearing this, immediately gave the merchant the slip, without waiting for his money, and, when the people found that he had fled, they pursued him to our camp; but our spies brought us timely notice of their approach, and we concealed our comrade beneath the trappings and housings of our horses. As soon as the enquiry was over, we quitted the neighbourhood of Elichpoor for a time, and afterwards, on returning, we found that a sedulous search was being made for the Nawab Subzi Kahn, by his son Sholam Hyder Kahn. He could be traced to Elichpoor, but no further. We immediately dispersed, and quitted that part of the country altogether."

The favourite haunt of these atrocious murderers, in the neighbourhood of Elichpoor, was an ancient and in great part dilapidated village called Mungrool,

Drawn by H. Warren from a Sketch by Capt. Meadows Taylor. Engraved by Finden.

Tomb of Meer Haiat Kulundur, Mungrool.

about half way between Elichpoor and Hingolee, under the little range of hills which bound the province of Berar, on the north. Here, the mausoleum of Meer Haiat Kalundur was a refuge for the miscreants, in cases of alarm; the officiating *fakhirs* having been accomplices if not actors in this trade of blood, until detected. From the assumed sanctity of their office, and the implicit confidence placed in them by unwary travellers who sought shelter in the tomb or in adjacent *serais*, these *fakhirs*, of course, enjoyed every possible facility for entrapping their prey. During the recent operations of the government for the suppression of *thuggi*, the remains of an appalling number of murdered persons were discovered in the neighbourhood, and many of the guilty blood-stained perpetrators were brought to execution, although befriended by the landholders as well as by the priests.

What rendered this abhorrent, inhuman system of *thuggi* peculiarly frightful in its nature and effect, was the wonderful secrecy with which its operations were carried on, notwithstanding the almost incredible extent to which all classes and characters of persons engaged in it; a religious secrecy, not inferior to that of free-masonry, and which, like that, had apparently existed for hundreds of years, without violation. It also possessed a mystic language of its own, by which the fraternity, like those of the masonic craft, were enabled to recognise and communicate with one another, without attracting the notice of the uninitiated. But enough has lately been written upon this subject to render a general description of the system unnecessary in this place; although it does not appear to be commonly known that even the most flourishing and wealthy merchants, as well as private individuals of otherwise irreproachable character, were, in numbers incredible, not only privy to, but actually practitioners of, the diabolical art. Captain Sleeman's reports mention an instance of a shopkeeper of excellent character, who had for several years served the officers and soldiers in cantonments, at Hingolee, being convicted as a leader of *thugs;* and persons of high rank have also been implicated in the practice. It is mentioned in the evidence of one culprit, that the *thugs* considered it their greatest security to be conspicuous persons, either in trade or office; as, in cases of discovery, the public would never think of looking for murderers among those whom they were accustomed to see daily, and to converse with, in so different a capacity. It is natural to suppose that intrepidity and boldness of demeanour would be the most valuable qualifications for the perpetration of such deeds of horror, and those best calculated to cover the criminals from detection; but these are qualities altogether unknown to the *thugs*, and they refer their long impunity to their characteristic timidity, which has driven them to unwearied caution. The

Hindoo goddess of evil, Kalli, is the presiding genius of *thuggi*, and under her banners, it is strange to relate, Mussulmans, no less than Hindoos, perform the bloody rites which they affect to regard as religious sacrifices. Yet when we find that the giant power of superstition has leagued itself with avarice, I know not how we can be surprised at any extremity of fiendish cruelty and guilt which may spring from the alliance.

The tomb of Meer Haiat Kalundur, at Mungrool, which I have mentioned as having been a favourite resort of these wretches, is thought to be of great antiquity; and it is probable, that the sanctified person whose name it records, accompanied into the Dekkan the army of Alla-ud-Deen, hereinbefore discoursed of. Little, however, is known concerning the history of his holiness, beyond what his name implies, and the anniversary of his death, on which day some honorary ceremonies are still observed, and a large *mela*, or fair, is held, for the purposes of worldly as well as of spiritual barter.

The term Kalundur,* is that which English translators have written calender, and which is pleasantly familiar to all lovers of the Arabian Nights' Entertainments. This tribe of religious mendicants is not numerous in India, doubtless in consequence of the slight esteem in which their community is here held, while in Arabia it still enjoys a high repute for

* The accent is on the second syllable.

sanctity. I have not, at any time, met with these people; but Captain Taylor, whose beautiful sketches are the chief embellishment of the present volume, has been more fortunate. He gives me the following note concerning them. "I have seen more of them at Hyderabad than elsewhere. Their costume is peculiar above all others. It consists of a conical felt hat, worked into chequers of white, red, and black; and their gown, which descends from the neck to the calf of the leg, is of diamond-shaped patches of the same colours. A few gourds for carrying water, are hung over the shoulder, or at the waist; and usually a bright steel rod, sometimes headed with a trident, completes their equipment. They never marry, but are of habits exceedingly dissolute and debauched, and are always most sturdy and importunate beggars." Stories of the kalundurs are current throughout India, and numerous enough to occupy another series of a thousand and one nights, though not always very creditable to the tribe. I have selected the following, as being illustrative of their pretensions to the especial favour and protection of Providence:—

THE KALUNDUR AND THE VIZIER.

In the days of religious prosperity, a kalundur, whose travel-worn appearance betokened his arrival from some distant place, made his salaam to the khalif, and demanded, in the name of Alla, to be admitted into the royal household, as the ghostly adviser of the court. The khalif was prepossessed by the kalundur's appearance, and not only granted his request, but promised to promote him to great favour, if his merits, and the nature of his services, were equal to his bold deportment. A short trial convinced the khalif of the superior wisdom and judgment of his new counsellor ; and, as his intelligence and accomplishments became daily more completely developed, the commander of the faithful evinced a growing preference for his society and conversation, and exhibited a marked deference to his opinions, such as he had never before been known to yield to any man. These things, of course, excited the envy of all the courtiers, and rendered the new-comer especially offensive to the vizier, whose glory was becoming daily more and more fully eclipsed. The kalundur still continued to increase in favour ; and the vizier, being afraid of taking open measures for his destruction, constrained himself to affect great cordiality of demeanour, in order that he might the more certainly effect his ruin by some secret stratagem.

With this motive, the vizier one day invited the kalundur to his house, to partake of a meal, previously to their evening attendance upon their royal master ; and, having received the kalundur's willing assent, he gave orders to his slaves to mix a large quantity of garlic with one half of each dish which was to be served up, and to place the dishes so that the portions containing the garlic should be nearest to his guest. The unsuspecting kalundur partook heartily of the savoury viands, and, when the meal was finished, complimented the vizier upon the skill of his cook.

"Truly," replied the wily vizier, "he has done his work most cleverly to-day; but it just occurs to me, that we have been indiscreet in indulging our appetites, to the prejudice of our duty towards the khalif. You perhaps were not aware, and I myself had until this moment forgotten, that he has a peculiar aversion to the scent of garlic; I fear, indeed, that he will scarcely tolerate our presence."

"Indeed, is it so?" said the kalundur, "how very untoward a circumstance is this! for the khalif informed me, after the *durbar*, that he should not be able to dispense with our attendance this evening, in consequence of some momentous affairs in which he required our united advice. However, with sound consciences, and a devout confidence in Alla and the prophet, we shall, doubtless, be relieved from all difficulties."

When the host and his guest had parted, the vizier went directly to the palace, and privately informed the khalif that the ungrateful kalundur had been guilty of treason, in disrespectfully circulating a report, that he, the commander of the faithful, had a breath so abominably impure and offensive, that it was past the endurance of all wholesome persons. Now, while the vizier was yet speaking, the kalundur entered the presence-chamber, and, having made his salaam, seated himself at a distance from the khalif, instead of at his usual post of distinction. This circumstance confirmed in the royal mind the truth of what the vizier had told him, but which he had hitherto regarded with suspicion. Hereupon the khalif commanded the kalundur to draw near. That faithful person immediately obeyed; but as he approached the throne, he very considerately covered his mouth with the sleeve of his garment, lest the scent of garlic should annoy the monarch. This second action put to flight all doubts which might have remained in the mind of the khalif, touching the accusation made against the kalundur; and the vizier, foreseeing, as he believed, a pending storm of rage and vengeance, silently withdrew, that he might appear to have taken no part in bringing about the downfal of the favourite. He was, however, but ill acquainted with the manners of his prince; for the khalif, restraining all expressions of the indignation which burnt within him, wrote on a slip of paper a few words to the governor of a distant fortress, saying:—"Let the bearer hereof be immediately put to such a death as may be a warning to all traitors." Having sealed it, the khalif delivered it to the kalundur, telling him to convey it to the governor to whom it was addressed, and to return speedily with an answer.

The kalundur, being ignorant of the purport of the letter with which he was entrusted, congratulated himself upon so ready an excuse for quitting his monarch's presence, without the necessity of opening his lips; and, making a humble salaam to the khalif, he withdrew. While he yet stood at the gate of the palace, preparing to mount his elephant, the vizier chanced to pass that way on horseback, and betrayed in his countenance no little astonishment on seeing the kalundur with his head still upon his shoulders. With affected concern, however, he inquired how that wise man had fortunately managed to escape the vengeance of the khalif.

The kalundur innocently replied,—"Alla and the Prophet befriended me; for although the khalif was evidently annoyed by the scent of the garlic, his great forbearance induced him to overlook my fault; probably in consideration of my careful delicacy in covering my mouth when I approached the royal presence. Nay, I have good cause to know that I have experienced no disfavour with my prince, inasmuch as he has entrusted me with an errand which will doubtless have its reward. One thing only perplexes me. I know not if the evil be attributable to the richness of your hospitality; but certain it is, that since I left the khalif, I have suffered so much internal pain, that I am doubtful of my ability to perform the journey."

The minister was undoubtedly mortified to find his scheme thus apparently frustrated; but his avarice taught him to anticipate some new advantage from the position of the kalundur. He expected that according to custom the messenger from the khalif would receive a munificent present from the governor of the fortress; and he also conjectured that if he could himself obtain the commission, a faithful and speedy execution of the khalif's orders might not only be rewarded with emolument, but also restore him to his former place and influence at court. Having revolved these things in his mind, the vizier exhibited the most affectionate regard for the kalundur's health, and entreated him, as a matter of duty to his sovereign, not to hazard his precious life by encountering the fatigues of travel at such a moment, but to suffer him, the vizier, to undertake the journey in his stead. The indisposition of the kalundur increased every moment, and as he feared to delay the royal commission with which he was charged, he reluctantly transferred his trust into the hands of the vizier, saying, "It is wisely written that the arrow of fate is always discharged from the bow of Providence; our lives are a mere target."

After the vizier had departed, the kalundur continued indisposed for several days, and was in consequence unable to attend the court; but the vizier, elate with his prospect of revenge and aggrandisement, proceeded to the governor's palace and delivered the khalif's letter. Immediately upon perusal of that death-warrant, the governor ordered the vizier to be bound with his head touching his heels, and in that posture to be suspended over the gate of the fort until he died; an inscription being written over him, warning all beholders that such would be the inevitable fate of all who should be guilty of perfidy or disrespect to a gracious sovereign.

It happened that, in the interim, the khalif also had been indisposed and unable to attend his court; but, on his recovery, he despatched a messenger to the house of the vizier, to inquire if any tidings had been received concerning the kalundur, or the object of his mission. The reply which he received was, that the kalundur was then in attendance upon his majesty's pleasure, with news of importance; but that the vizier had been some days departed upon his majesty's commission to the governor of a certain distant fortress. On hearing these things, the khalif was filled with admiration, for with the eagle eye of wisdom he in a moment detected the operation of Divine justice. The kalundur was immediately admitted to the presence, and a few words of explanation sufficed to establish the truth of the reflection which the kalundur had addressed to the vizier: "The arrow of fate is always discharged from the bow of Providence; our lives are a mere target."

GAWILGHUR AND MOOHKTAGHENI.

War, my lord,
Is of eternal use to humankind.

JEFFERY.

About twenty miles distant from Elichpoor, in the direction of Boorhanpoor, is Gawilghur, lately one of the strongest hill-fortresses in Southern India. The citadel crowns a lofty rugged cone projecting from the chain of mountains which bounds the province of Berar on the north; and the fortifications extend in three distinct lines of irregular works, around all the angles of its precipitous sides. Whether its natural or artificial defences be most formidable, it is difficult to decide. The place is of great antiquity; it has been described by Abul Fazil under the name of Kaweel, and other historians have called it Gavul and Gaial. The natives affirm that it was originally built by one of the earliest of the monarchs of Delhi, but that, having fallen into decay, it was rebuilt by Mahmood Gawan, at the command of Mohummed Shah the Second. This notion has probably arisen from an anecdote in the history of Mohummed Shah, related by Ferishta, concerning some fort which must have been situated hereabouts, but of which the name is not mentioned. "Mohummed Shah," says this entertaining historian, "happening one day to be marching by a ruined hill-fort, inquired its origin, and the cause of its neglected fate. Being told that it had been erected by an ancient king of Delhi to keep the borderers in subjection, the prince halted, and commanded that it should be repaired without delay, entrusting the execution of his orders to his general Mahmood Gawan. This chief made such wonderful exertions, that the ordinary work of two years was accomplished in the short space of six months, a garrison was established, and ample stores of all kinds were laid in for its defence. Mohummed Shah, finding the work completed in so short a time, exclaimed, 'The omnipotent Alla hath bountifully conferred upon me two incalculable blessings—a great kingdom, and a still greater servant!' Thus saying, he took off his upper robes, and bidding Mahmood Gawan receive and wear them, he took, in their place, those of the fortunate Mahmood Gawan, and put them on his own person. No history, perhaps, records an instance of so extraordinary an honour conferred by any king upon a subject." This tale, it must be allowed, is, at best, a little doubtful in its application, although certain it is that great improvements and enlargements were made in the place by Mohummed Shah, and that after he had subdivided the province of Berar into two governments, Gawilghur became one of the capitals.

It may be mentioned, as an instance of the precarious value of a despot's highest favour, that the active, devoted servant whom Mohummed Shah thus distinguished, very shortly afterwards suffered an unjust death at the hand of his prince, upon the bare accusation of some envious conspirators. An inscription was placed over his remains, which, by a play upon the numeral letters contained in the date of his death, records the injustice of his fate. It is thus written :—

If you would know the date whereupon the innocent martyr, truly worthy of profound veneration, whose unmeasured bounty made the whole earth to rejoice, first drank the black waters of eternity, you will find it commemorated in

قتل نا حق

The unjust Execution.

In Numerals.

The fifth day of the month Suffur, A. H. 886.

The historian above quoted relates the incident by which this faithful vizier acquired his name, Gawan, which signifies "a cow." Mohammed Shah was one evening seated upon the *chubootra*, or marble terrace, in front of the palace, surrounded by his nobles and officers of state, enjoying the fragrant fumes of his hookka and the witty converse of his familiars, among whom the vizier was pre-eminent. Presently in the midst of their mirth a cow commenced lowing and making a great noise, immediately beneath the terrace ; when one of the assembly laughingly inquired, " O vizier, being undoubtedly an oracle of wisdom, you will certainly be able to inform us what that cow is talking about." To which the vizier immediately replied : " The cow was addressing herself to me only ; but, as you desire to know the meaning of her discourse, I will not withhold it, since it may be found instructive. She spoke in terms of remonstrance, saying, ' O vizier! wherefore, being one of my species, do you degrade yourself and your kind, by holding communion with asses?' " All present trembled for the presumption of the minister, but Mohammed Shah, as the vizier had foreseen, was too well amused by the readiness of his wit to be angry, and only imposed upon him the cognomen of Gawan, to commemorate the circumstance.

The fortress of Gawilghur experienced many reverses of fortune during the short-lived dynasty of the Imad Shahi kings of Berar, who threw off their allegiance to the princes of Bidur in A.D. 1484. It was in this place that the usurper Toofal Kahn took refuge with his young son and a little band of faithful adherents, after his army had been routed and literally annihilated by the king of Ahmednuggur. Pursued to the very walls of the fort by a party of the enemy's cavalry, he was actually overtaken by the foremost horseman at the very gate; and, exhausted with fatigue, he would doubtless have fallen, an easy captive, into the hands of his pursuers, had it not been but for the assistance of a woman who, having anxiously watched his flight from the battlement, became interested in his fate, although a stranger to her, and effected his rescue by casting down, upon the head of the trooper, a heavy stone, which killed him upon the spot.

The impregnable nature of the fortress rendered Toofal Kahn a temporary security against the arms of his foes; and when his little garrison was reduced to a feeble band of only a dozen men, he still managed, for a time, to keep his assailants at bay. After great labour and perseverance, however, the besiegers succeeded in dragging a gun up the mountain's side to a spot whence they could batter one of the bastions; and having, by degrees, effected a practicable breach, an officer, with twenty-eight men and a trumpeter, secretly, under cover of the night, surmounted the wall. Having gained the ramparts, the gallant leader ordered the trumpeter to blow a loud blast, and the affrighted garrison, believing that a large force had surprised them, abandoned the fort, without striking a blow, and fled to the neighbouring mountains. Toofal Kahn was shortly afterwards captured, with his family and a small band of his followers—amounting in all to about forty persons; they were inhumanly crammed into a small dungeon, a miniature of the Calcutta black-hole, where they all perished in a few hours. Gawilghur continued for many years the seat of government for Berar, although the princes frequently resided at Elichpoor, and at a palace, about four miles distant from the fort, prettily called Kahnsamankanuggur.

A few words concerning the last assault which Gawilghur sustained, will possibly prove more acceptable to English readers than all the tales of its vicissitudes, from the time of the very first Mohummed; for undoubtedly an especial interest will be attached to information which is in any measure illustrative of the Despatches of his Grace the Duke of Wellington, lately published. I have refrained from attempting any particular description of the plan and disposition of the fortress, in order that I might avail myself of the words of the illustrious personage who conducted the operations alluded to. The Duke of Wellington (then Major-General the Honourable Arthur Wellesley) invested Gawilghur on the 13th of December 1803, thirteen days after his glorious victory of Argaum; and in his despatch to the Governor-General, he gives the following account of the place:—

"The fort of Gawilghur is situated in a range of mountains between the sources of the rivers Poorna and Taptee. It stands on a lofty mountain in this range, and consists of one complete inner fort which fronts to the south, where the rock is most steep, and an outward fort which covers the inner to the north-west and north. This outer fort has a third wall, which covers the approach to it from the north by the village of Labada. All these walls are strongly built and fortified by ramparts and towers. The communications with the fort are through three gates; one to the south with the inner fort; one to the north with the outer fort; and one to the north with the third wall. The ascent to the first is very long and steep, and is practicable only for men; that to the second is by a road used for the common communications of the garrison with the countries southward; but the road passes round the west side of the fort, and is exposed for a great distance to its fire: it is so narrow as to make it impracticable to approach regularly by it, and the rock is scarped on each side. This road also leads no farther than to the gate. The communication with the northern gate is direct from the village of Labada, and here the ground is level with that of the fort; but the road to Labada leads through the mountains, about thirty miles from Elichpoor, and it was obvious that the difficulty and labour of moving ordnance and stores to Labada would be very great. However, after making inquiry at Elichpoor, it appeared both to Colonel Stevenson and me that this point of attack was upon the whole the most advantageous, and we accordingly adopted it."

Such were the outward difficulties of this fastness, defended by a brave and skilful commander, Benee Singh, with a garrison of five thousand hardy Rajhpoots and Ghoseins, in addition to irregulars; and yet, within eight-and-forty hours from the opening of their batteries, the British troops had stormed and carried the fort. But, fortunately, with British troops and British commanders, increased difficulties only give rise to renewed ardour and determination. The illustrious Duke occupied the ground in front of the southern face, through which pass the only roads communicating with the plains. Another division, commanded by Colonel Stevenson, by dint of perseverance against difficulties almost insurmountable, succeeded in dragging a battering train through ravines and mountain torrents, to the table-land overlooking the northern side. From this point the main assault was made, while the garrison was diverted by feints upon the south and north-west gates. After the breaches were reported practicable, the storming party, gallantly commanded by Lieut.-Colonel Kenny, carried it like true British soldiers, though opposed in the most determined manner by Benee Singh, in person, supported by the Killadar and a strong force of chosen men; all of whom, including their leaders, fell sword in hand, having solemnly sworn that they would die rather than submit. The second wall being deeply retired, could not be breached by either battery, but was carried by escalade in the most spirited manner, by a detachment from the light company of the 94th Regt., under Captain Campbell. These, having surmounted the wall, cut their way to the gate in defiance of all resistance, and succeeded in opening it to the storming party, who instantly rushed in and took possession of the fort. The greater part of the garrison who were not slain, expecting no quarter, leaped from the battlements, and were dashed to atoms. The spot where Benee Singh and his brave followers were cut down is marked by a few humble tombs, which the Rajhpoots point out with much pride. Although in the thoroughfare from the Delhi gate, they might otherwise escape the notice of a stranger, so unpretending are they in appearance; while they are surrounded, on all sides, with the ostentatious mausoleums of proud Mussulmans, whose very names have long since passed into oblivion.

Before Benee Singh went to the defence of the breach, he had told his wife that he had vowed not to outlive the fall of the place, and had exacted from her a promise, that if his signet were brought to her, which would be a token of his death, she should immediately destroy herself; and in the same event he commanded all the women of his household to be put to death, according to the Rajhpoot custom in such cases. When the Duke entered the fort, he found these poor women, twelve or fourteen in number, some dead and others severely wounded, huddled together at the bottom of a dry reservoir, weltering in their blood. Those who survived were tenderly taken care of, and, much to their astonishment, were restored with all possible respect to such friends as chanced to remain to them. A boy, a son of the Killadar's, was also found severely wounded; and after he recovered, the Duke bestowed upon him some villages beyond the hills, where he still resides, losing no opportunity of extolling to the skies the very wonderful and unexpected generosity of the conqueror.

Colonel Welsh, who was present at the investment of Gawilghur, tells an amusing and characteristic anecdote, exhibiting a fair specimen of the material of which British veterans are composed. He says: "We had been one night working very hard at a battery half way up the hill, and afterwards cleared a road up to it; but no power we possessed could move our iron battering-guns above a few hundred yards from the bottom, so steep and rugged was the ascent. I had just been relieved from working by a fresh party, and was enjoying a few moments' rest on some clean straw, when the officer commanding the working party came up to Colonel Wallace, and reported that it was impossible to get the heavy guns up to the battery. The Colonel, who was brigadier of the trenches, exclaimed,—'Impossible! hoot,

Painted by T. Creswick from a Sketch by Capt. Meadows Taylor. Engraved by Finden.

Pan Puttah Gate, [illegible]

London. Published Oct. 1. 1839, by Charles Tilt, 86 Fleet Street.

mon! it must be done! I've got the order in my pocket!' These words, although they failed to transport the guns into the battery, fully illustrated the true character of this noble and devoted soldier."

The result of the assault of Gawilghur was a death-blow to the hopes of the chiefs who had confederated to oppose the British government, and was immediately followed by a treaty of peace, which did honour to the generosity no less than to the diplomacy of the great General who arranged it.

The Peer Putteh Gate, which is represented in the annexed view, stands at the top of a rugged and difficult acclivity, which is called the Short Ghat, because somewhat less rugged and difficult than the others. The traveller who accomplishes the ascent is, however, amply recompensed for his labour, by the magnificent scenery spread out on all sides around him, and by the cool, refreshing air, which is the more enjoyable when contrasted with the close, unwholesome vapours of the ravines and jungul passes of the low country. On either side of the gateway is a watch-tower, containing many small rooms, with embrasures which overlook the fortifications; these were formerly used as places of arms. Surmounting the tower on the right is a spacious apartment, which, from the superiority of its finish, appears to have been the resort of the chieftains, and, when in repair, must have afforded them a delightful evening lounge. Over the entrance is a Persian inscription, which states that the gate was erected by Sultan Mahmood: unfortunately the date is obliterated. There are two or three other ruins of interest in the fort; but, since the siege, it has been very thinly inhabited, and allowed to fall into complete dilapidation. The Jumma Musjid, or principal mosque, is in a rapid process of decay, but still occasionally used by the faithful for the performance of worship. There are some fine remains of the old Rajh Mahal, or royal palace, a Mohummedan structure of great extent; but many of the walls, as well as the roof, have fallen, and are now overrun with rank weeds of gigantic growth and jungul grass: an enticing cover for the bears, leopards, jackals, and lesser animals, which are here very numerous, and appear to share such accommodation as the fort offers, upon a most amicable understanding with the other inhabitants. Terry, that quaintest of early travellers to India, gives an amusing account of the "discommodities, inconveniences, and annoyances," arising from the multitude of wild beasts and vermin which frequently disturb the habitations of man in the East. "The annoyances of these countries," he writes, "are, first, many harmful beasts of prey, such as lyons, tygers, woolves, jackalls, with others. Those jackalls seem to be wild dogs, who in great companies run up and down in the silent night, much disquieting the peace thereof, by their most hideous noise. Those most ravenous creatures will not suffer a man to rest quietly in his grave even; for, if his body be not buried very deep, they will dig him thence, and bury as much of him again as they can consume in their hungry bellies. In their rivers are many crocodiles, and—*latet anguis in herba*—on the land not a few overgrown snakes, with other venomous and pernicious creatures." Could Terry return to his earthly wanderings, and take up his abode for a few days among the ruins of Gawilghur, it is possible that he might be induced to form as charitable an opinion of the jackals and other harmful beasts of prey, as he ultimately did concerning the lizards, which he has described as being "shaped likely unto crocodiles, of a sad green colour, and but little creatures, the fear of whom presents itself mostly to the eye; for," says he, "I do not know of a certainty that they are in anywise hurtful." The natives of Gawilghur affirm, that notwithstanding the great numbers of these formidable fellow-citizens, they are never so "abundantly disquieted by the ferocity and rapaciousness of them" as was the "heart-affrightened" Terry.

There are the remains of many extensive tanks or reservoirs within the fort. Some of them are still filled with water, and must have been remarkably handsome, when in repair, especially that called the Deo Talab, pool of Mahadeo, who is the tutelar god of the place, under the name of Bulla-ji. Upon an eminence near the Deo Talab is a pretty little temple dedicated to this deity, containing a row of white marble images, with the usual multiplicity of arms, and hideousness of aspect; but these impersonations of the god's attributes are now neglected in consequence of an event whereby, a few years since, the altars became polluted. The story, by way of distinction, is called

THE TRAGEDY OF GAWILGHUR,

and is thus told:—

The officiating Brahmin was a very aged and infirm man, but renowned for his great sanctity and the efficacy of his prayers. During a life of extreme privation and self-denial, the old man had succeeded in amassing a very large sum of money, which it was expected he would eventually bequeath for the rebuilding or repairing of all sacred Hindoo edifices within the fort. One evening a Gossein arrived at Gawilghur, travel-worn and exhausted; and, having been cherished and refreshed by the hospitality and anxious care of the pious Hindoos whose charity he claimed, he inquired, as a stranger, for the temple of Mahadeo, and presently retired thither. He remained many days at the temple, assisting the Brahmin in his religious duties, to all appearance a most devoted and indefatigable slave of the god.

So excellent and useful a person did this Gossein appear, that he was received into great favour and confidence by the Brahmin, and was entrusted to levy contributions on the inhabitants, for the service of the temple, in an approaching festival. It was generally understood that at this pageant in honour of their tutelar god, the devout Gossein would publicly submit to some wonderfully excruciating penance and mortification; and it therefore excited no little surprise in the minds of the guards, when, on the morning before the festival, they beheld the stranger, equipped as if for a journey, attempt to pass out by the southern gate. His manner, too, excited suspicion, and it was noticed that his feet were bespattered with blood. Being questioned by the Durwan, he replied that, being a Jhain, and not an orthodox Hindoo, he had just been preparing a ram for sacrifice, and was then bound in search of certain herbs which could be found only in the plains: but the confusion of his demeanour, and the apparently great weight of the bundle which he carried over his shoulder, induced the Durwan to detain the holy man, in defiance of his protestations and anathemas. Finding resistance vain, he was, at his own request, taken back to the temple, to prove, as he said, the truth of his assertions.

On entering the apartment, the guard discovered a spectacle which filled the hearts of all beholders with utter consternation and horror. Prostrate before the altar, with the head towards the principal image of the god, as if in the act of prayer, lay the lifeless form of the aged Brahmin, his skull literally beaten to atoms, and his brains scattered about the floor. Beside him lay a small marble image of the god, besmeared with blood, and which had evidently been used as the implement of murder. Terror-stricken at this awful sight—for Menu has declared the murder of a Brahmin to be the most inexpiable of all crimes, and one which brings the vengeance of Heaven upon the very soil itself, and upon all dwellers in the neighbourhood where the deed is perpetrated, no less than upon the murderer—the Durwan and the rest of the guard fell upon their faces to implore the protection of the insulted god; and at that moment the culprit, taking advantage of the confusion, fled from the temple and leaped over the battlements. Down, down, he was hurled, about a hundred and fifty feet, over the rugged precipice, expecting to terminate his flight in the waters of the reservoir below; but as the all-knowing Mahadeo had purposely broken away the embankment and drawn off the water, in the night-time, the murderous Gossein was plunged headforemost into soft mud, in which he sunk up to his blood-stained feet. He was immediately rescued, though in an insensible state, by some persons who, from below, had witnessed his headlong fall; and, before he was restored to consciousness, he was again in the custody of the guards.

He now made a full confession of his crime, and an enormous amount of the Brahmin's treasure was found in his bundle, and in secret places where he had concealed it. Without further trial, he was loaded with heavy irons, and condemned to carry large stones for the rebuilding of the walls. But his earthly punishment was not of long duration; for the vengeful Mahadeo afflicted him with a dreadful leprosy, besides a hundred other infirmities; and he speedily sank under a horrible accumulation of mental and bodily pangs. Although, in his life-time, no clue could be obtained to his former history, it was discovered, after his death, that he was the son of a wealthy Hindoo merchant at Boorhanpoor, who, some years previously, had been compelled to cast him off, for his incorrigible profligacy.

The hills about Gawilghur have for ages past been a favourite retreat for that extraordinary sect, the Jhains; concerning whom scarcely any authentic information is on record. They, in many respects, resemble the ancient Boodhists: several of their tenets are similar; their temples are frequently of the same fashion; and their images of worship are remarkable for the curly hair and African features peculiar to the Boodhist idols. These two sects agree in denying the divine origin of the Vedas; they follow a similar mode of worship, in honour of certain eminent saints having the same attributes, though they are differently named; and they mutually recognize the subordinate deities of the orthodox Hindoos. With both, the doctrine of transmigration is essential. Their legendary tales and mystical allegories, though differing in substance, are wonderfully similar, in tone and character, and even surpass in exaggeration the monstrous absurdities of Brahminical Hindooism. In all other matters, the Jhains and the Boodhists are at variance, especially with regard to caste; for although the Jhains admit the usual division into the four principal tribes, they select their priests from the *Bhaisias* or cultivators, instead of from the Brahmins. This has, according to the earliest traditions, given undying offence to the Brahmins, who are ever at open warfare with the Jhains; and in consequence of this, the latter are always found in separate communities. Among some classes of Brahmins, this spirit of enmity is carried to so great a length that they introduce into their daily prayer the most bitter maledictions against the Jhains; and these again, for the sake of retaliation, habitually cry out "*Brahmuni Kshaium*," that is, "May the Brahmins perish!"

The Jhain temples may be known more by the peculiarity of their sculptures than by any singularity or uniformity of structure; and they are usually found in groups of eight, or ten, or more, huddled closely together in some very retired and romantic spot. The accompanying drawing represents some remarkable specimens, situated upon the precipitous banks of a mountain torrent, at a place called Moohktagherri, a little distance north-west from Gawilghur. The spot whereon these temples stand is remarkably picturesque. It is approached by a narrow winding path, beside a mountain-torrent which dashes through the bottom of a thickly wooded glen; whence a peep may, here and there, be caught of the temples, towering aloft, and overhung by a wildly precipitous and craggy mountain, from the rugged sides whereof, numerous foaming cataracts gush forth. Now, uniting in one broad expanse, a rolling mass of foam goes tumbling headlong from a giddy height, and spreads a silver mist across the hanging woods, amid which a thousand mimic rainbows appear and vanish with magical rapidity, as the eddying breezes continually assemble and disperse. And now again a boldly jutting rock divides and scatters wide the foaming tide, which creeps away in a hundred bubbling rills, here lost in brakes and underwood, here glistening forth in the bright sunshine, and there gliding stealthily through the soft green moss, to mix with other gathering streams, again to bound away over the downward precipice.

From the lowest fall, the ascent to the temples is accomplished by means of a long and difficult flight of broken steps, sometimes cut in the rock, and elsewhere formed by a large loose stone or two, which a careless foot may send plunging into the boiling abyss below. These steps are terminated at the top by a narrow archway, under which the pathway leads, turning sharp round the salient angle of the mountain; and hence a new scene of enchantment opens upon the sight. On a level terrace in the mountain's side are ten or eleven lofty temples, of various forms and colours, some brilliantly white, others of all the warm gradations of red and brown, perched on high over the rushing cataract, which here falling about sixty feet, thunders upon the sloping sides of the mountain below, and shakes the very ground on which the buildings stand. From the edge of the precipice the foaming waters may be seen roaring down the steep descent, until they hurry through a blackened, gloomy archway; and from thence, emerging on the other side, they once more roll away down their rocky course, and dashing beneath a perilous-looking bridge at the bottom, they meet the waters of the other falls in a large deep pool, skirted around with gigantic forest-trees.

These temples are apparently very ancient; more so, probably, than the idols within them, upon one of which a Sanskrit inscription is carved, assigning to them a date coinciding pretty nearly with the Norman invasion of England. The sculptures everywhere around are rude, but full of energy; and, notwithstanding the moisture of the place, and their exposed position, appear likely to remain as many centuries as they have already stood. Near the

Drawn by H. Warren, from a Sketch by Capt. Meadows Taylor. Engraved by Finden.

Jaina Temples, Mooktagheree.

London, Published Oct. 1, 1839, by Charles Tilt, 86, Fleet Street.

temples are the remains of a *serai*, and also an extensive ruin, which has evidently been used, or intended for, a monastery, being divided into numerous narrow cells, with here and there a remnant of sculpture, emblematic of the office of the ancient occupant.

At the bottom of the upper fall, and sufficiently near to be continually wetted by the water, is a small archway of gothic form, hewn in the solid rock. This is the entrance to a little excavated chapel, apparently of a later date than the buildings, it being profusely ornamented with Saracenic carvings, and roofed with goins and intersecting arches, which spring from elegant pillars of the Moorish style. The apartment is very small, and, from want of ventilation, the air within is so abominably offensive, that even the most curious visitor will make but a hasty survey of it. Foul birds, bats, vampires, and noxious reptiles, have for many years past made it their abode, attracted by its darkness and the chilly damps which cling to and exude from its slimy sides. Just within the entrance, the incessant fulminations of the cataract are perfectly deafening; the loudest shout, even the bark of a dog, can scarcely be heard. The place, though elegant in form, is fraught with horrors to the mind; indeed, imagination can hardly picture a scene possessing so extraordinary a combination of the beautiful and attractive, with the utterly repulsive and disgusting. All unpleasant images may here, however, be speedily banished from the mind. Every turn, like a movement of the kaleidoscope, presents the beholder with a new and ever-changing scene. The wildest and the homeliest are equally varied and equally beautiful, and on all sides court the admiration of the visitor ;—for here, in truth, it may be said that—

> Mighty nature bounds as from her birth ;
> The sun is in the heavens and life on earth,
> Flowers in the valley, splendour in the beam,
> Health on the gale, and freshness in the stream.

It was in some sequestered nook, among the flowery solitudes of these wild mountains, that, peaceful, and undisturbed by

> The fall of kings,
> The rage of nations and the crush of states,

there lived, and died at the age of a hundred years, the holy Parswanauth, the twenty-third deified saint, and probably the founder of the Jhaina tribe ; in honour of whom most of the Jhain temples are said to be erected, and whom the colossal figures usually attached to them are supposed to represent. Most of the glorious deeds of this Parswanauth, during his mortal life, are concealed in profound mystery, or else are too sacred to be imparted to the ears of heretics ; for nothing more than what is here told of him can be learnt, except that the place of his birth was in the suburbs of Benares; whence he removed, while yet a child, disgusted at the inconsistencies of the Brahminical faith.

Besides these temples at Moohktagherri, there are but few works of the Jhains in central India. The most remarkable are near the village of Seravana Belgala, in the kingdom of Mysore, where, besides excavations, and conical temples hewn from the solid rock, there is a gigantic figure formed of a single stone, seventy feet in height, called Gautama Raia, which, some years since, the Duke of Wellington narrowly examined, and supposes to have been wrought by cutting away the substance of the hill on which it stands, until nothing but the image and its pedestal remained,—a plan which has apparently been frequently adopted by the Hindoos.

The most striking peculiarity which appertains to the religious profession of the Jhains, is the ridiculous extent to which they carry their scruples respecting the destruction of animal life. Their absurdities in this matter are far beyond those of the Hindoos. With one exception,—the sacrifice of the ram,—they esteem the destruction of any sentient creature, however minute, as the most heinous of crimes; and continually carry at their girdles a small broom, suspended by a string, with which they tenderly sweep aside every insect which they may observe in their path, lest they should accidentally tread upon it. To so senseless a length do they carry this principle, that they will not pluck any herb or vegetable, or partake of any sort of food, which may be supposed to contain animalculi; so that the only articles of sustenance remaining to them appear to be rice, and a few sorts of pulse, which they cook with milk. They affirm, indeed, that it is as foul a murder to kill an insect as to slay a man; and so extreme is their precaution to avoid the commission of the crime, that it is with great reluctance, and only when reduced to the necessity by urgent thirst, that they will drink water; even then, they invariably suck up the fluid through a piece of fine muslin. In like manner, when they require water for ablution, or any unavoidable household purpose, they carefully strain it repeatedly, before they venture to use it. The most noxious vermin and insects are also treated with the same consideration as the most harmless creatures; and if, through persevering annoyance, they are compelled to deprive certain odious insects of the asylum usually found upon their persons, they remove the tormentors with the utmost care, and tenderly place them out of harm's way.

The highest distinction to which the sanctity of a Jhaina devotee can advance him, is styled Saniasi Nirvani, nude penitent, and is attained only by a long course of extreme penance, and the most rigid observance of the laws of the order. In this sublime state, the soul is supposed to be partially absorbed into the essence of the Divinity, and the man becomes almost insensible to earthly concerns. He is said to be devoid of all human passions, and acknowledges none of the requirements of nature; hunger and thirst are unknown to him; abstruse contemplation is his only sleep; heat and cold, disease and infirmity, alike fail to inflict pain or inconvenience; and his eye rests with equal indifference upon good and evil. Being divested of all wants, he lives in absolute independence of his one-time fellow mortals, and estranges himself from all communion with them, having no thought, affection, or inclination, except for things divine. In this manner, he advances, step by step, in purity and excellence, during which time the principles or elements of his natural body are gradually dissolved, until, having passed through eleven intermediate stages, he arrives at ultimate perfection, and becomes inseparably united with the Deity.

It is not possible for any person among the Jhains to attain the high and sublime order of Saniasi Nirvani, at pleasure; because he cannot be qualified with the necessary degree of purity, unless he has already passed through some millions of transmigrations.

BOORHANPOOR.

———History, with all her volumes vast,
Hath but one page.

THIS city stands on the north-west side of the river Tupti, and commands the most extensive and fruitful plains in the province of Kandeish, of which it is the ancient capital. It is one of the largest, and perhaps the best-built, of the cities in the Dekkan, and enjoys a foremost importance in wealth, as a commercial and manufacturing city. Moreover its consequence is not confined to mere matters of fact; for it possesses very abundant interest for the traveller, as a treasury of antiquarian remains, and as the scene of many stirring and tragical events, connected with the history of the Mogul power in these provinces. The place was founded in A. D. 1416, by Nazur Khan, of the Farooki dynasty, and was called Boorhanpoor, in honour of the great and learned—afterwards sainted—Sheik Boorhan-ud-Deen, (chief of the faithful). The circumstances which gave rise to the building of the city are ripe with romantic incident, and give additional interest to its subsequent history. They are thus told in

Drawn by W. Warren, from a Sketch by Capt. Meadows Taylor

Engraved by S. Fisher

Near Boorhanpoor, Aseer Ghur in the distance.

THE LEGEND OF ASA AHEER.

Upon the summit of a high hill, about twelve miles from the spot on which Boorhanpoor now exhibits its giddy towers and circling domes, there stood, in ancient times, the habitation of a herdsman; whose ancestors, through untold generations, had enjoyed peaceful possession of the soil of the mountain, from its summit to its base. In the reign of Moolluk Raja, the first of the sovereigns of Kandeish, about A.D. 1365, this little territory was held by Asa Aheer, (Asa the cow-herd), who is said to have possessed records and traditions of his forefathers, extending over a period of seven hundred years. Yet was not Asa Aheer inferior in wisdom or benevolence to any of his family who had gone before him, and the flourishing condition of the estate was a living proof of their skill and prudence: for by dint of industry and good management, from generation to generation, the family had raised themselves from poverty to the enjoyment of great agricultural wealth and influence. Asa Aheer, having greatly improved and extended the habitations and defences upon the mountain, gave it the name of Aseer, a familiar corruption of his patronymic; and, after a few years of careful toil and well-applied diligence, he found himself possessed of retainers, of herds, and treasure, ten-fold of his original inheritance: indeed it is recorded that he numbered five thousand buffaloes, five thousand cows, twenty thousand sheep, and a thousand brood-mares; and that the number of his multiplied family and dependants, who were employed in defence of the property against marauders, as well as in agricultural labour, amounted to no less than two thousand able-bodied men, besides thousands of women and children.

Pride and contumely, the common attendants of good-fortune, had no place in the presence of Asa Aheer; for, with excellence of understanding, he possessed excellence of heart, and, like each of his forefathers, was esteemed as a chief and protector by all the neighbouring herdsmen. Whether advice only, or more substantial assistance, might be required, neither one nor the other was ever sought in vain from Asa Aheer: his ear was ever open to the voice of distress, his hand ever ready to bestow relief; so that some of all classes of his neighbours were continually flying to him in cases of difficulty and misfortune. A noble specimen of his munificence and goodness of heart occurred at the close of Moolluk Raja's reign, which raised him to the highest pitch of popularity and esteem. A fearful famine had carried devastation and death through all the neighbouring countries, reducing many of the wealthiest to abject poverty, and sweeping thousands of the poor into eternity, so that scarcely one-third of the inhabitants survived. Asa Aheer was at this time possessed of a very great number of stores and granaries, in the districts round about Aseer, so that all persons were calculating the enormous gains which would, in consequence of this public calamity, be rolled into the treasury of a single individual. His friends congratulated him upon his prospect of becoming the greatest and wealthiest subject in the Dekkan; but Asa Aheer, quietly rebuking them for their evil opinion of him, made them the bearers of orders to all his agents to supply the wants of the poor without price; to sell grain to the middle classes, who could afford to pay, at the usual rate; and, from the wealthy, to demand fourfold of what was paid by others, and to distribute the three-fourths overcharged in alms. In order to find employment for those who were strong enough to labour, he caused all the buildings and defences upon the hill of Aseer to be thrown down, and rebuilt in a much more costly and substantial manner. It is even said that, in person, he attended the dying; and, with his own hand, distributed food and clothing to the aged and infirm: yet not, as some, from ostentation or the love of adulation, but from pure compassion for his suffering fellow-countrymen.

Notwithstanding the acquisition of his great wealth and authority, Asa Aheer was a peaceful and unambitious subject; and, upon the accession of Moolluk Raja, had been among the foremost to acknowledge his duty, and to perform his fealty to his lawful sovereign, presenting that prince with many valuable tokens of his submission and respect. Hence Moolluk Raja manifested no jealousy towards him; although he was fain to observe that so impregnable a stronghold as that of Aseer, in the very centre of his kingdom, would place any monarch at the mercy of its possessor, had he been an unruly or ambitious man. Moolluk Raja died, and was succeeded on the *musnud* by Nazur Kahn, and to him also Asa Aheer hastened to perform his homage, accompanying it with substantial proofs of his sincerity. But although Nazur Kahn, knowing the kindly disposition of the herdsman chief, felt himself perfectly secure from any evil design on his part, he was led away by avarice and jealousy to plot his downfal. So true is the proverb, that "although a rug will accommodate ten dervishes, yet the largest kingdom is insufficient for two rulers." This crafty prince, observing that the peaceable and blameless conduct of Asa Aheer would supply him with no pretext for accusation or open assault, determined upon gaining Aheer by stratagem; and for the purpose of carrying his base design into effect, he had recourse to the following expedient, forgetting, doubtless, that a much smaller measure of duplicity would have sufficed to circumvent his unsuspicious victim.

The prince wrote a complimentary letter to Asa

Aheer, informing him that the Rajas of Buglana and Antoor had assembled large bodies of armed men, for the purpose of disputing his authority, and that they had already threatened a descent upon his capital. He represented that the fortress of Talnere had, by virtue of his father's will, been placed in the hands of his brother Mooluk Iftikhar, with whom he was at enmity; that his hereditary enemy, the raja of Kehrla, had renewed hostilities, and that Lulling, which was the only fort strong enough to offer him a safe retreat, was situated too far from the centre of his dominions. He therefore entreated that Asa Aheer would afford his family a refuge within the walls of Aseer. To this request Asa Aheer returned a cheerful welcome; and, expressing himself sensible of the high honour conferred upon him, begged that his sovereign would be pleased to appropriate, as far as they were worthy of so great a prince, all the possessions and comforts which he could offer. He immediately gave orders for extensive preparations to be made for a suitable reception of the royal visitors; and especially directed that every possible luxury and convenience should be provided for the ladies. With very little delay, the treacherous Nazur Kahn availed himself of the herdsman's simplicity, and sent forward about fifty palanquins, containing females of the royal household. These had orders to report to Asa Aheer that they came to be in readiness for the royal party, who might be expected on the following morning. Accordingly, ere the sun had risen next day, news was brought that four hundred palanquins belonging to the prince were approaching, and immediately Asa Aheer ordered the gates of his fort to be thrown open, while he and his family went into the bazaar to meet their illustrious visitors. Scarcely had the last palanquin been admitted within the gates, when, at a signal from the captain who commanded the body-guard, every palanquin was thrown open; and each was found to contain two armed soldiers, who forthwith leaped out, and commenced an indiscriminate slaughter of all the inhabitants—indiscriminate, except inasmuch as the venerable Asa Aheer and every member of his family were marked for immediate destruction,—men, women, and children, even to the youngest babe, so that not one of the race remained. Those of the inhabitants who were spared fled with terror from their homes, and left the hill entirely in the occupation of their enemies.

Nazur Kahn, who during the massacre had remained in the fort of Lulling, no sooner heard of the success of his diabolical treachery, than he repaired to Aseer; and having peopled it with his own creatures, he greatly extended and improved the town and fortifications, having determined to make it his own abode and the capital of his kingdom.

At this time, the chief priests and guardians of Nazur Kahn were Sheik Zein-ud-Deen and Sheik

Boorhan-ud-Deen; both of them men of great repute in learning and religion, and principals of the Madressa, or college, at Dowlutabad. To these men Nazur Kahn sent the news of his glorious victory; and they immediately set forth towards Kandeish, in order to congratulate the prince upon his success against a powerful family of an inimical faith, or, to use their own words, "a nest of poisonous infidels."

Nazur Kahn, with all his family, marched to meet these holy fathers, and encamped on the western bank of the river Tupti, at the very same moment that the two sheiks were pitching their tents on the eastern bank; but these latter being under an obligation not to cross the river, received the visits of the prince in their own tents. Nazur Kahn tried with great perseverance to persuade them to return with him to Aseer, but they were not to be prevailed upon, even by promises of money; so that, after both parties had remained a few days encamped in their original positions, they prepared to return home. Once more Nazur Kahn earnestly endeavoured to purchase the attendance of his spiritual counsellors, offering each of them a noble *jaghir* in Kandeish; but they replied that they sought neither wealth nor dominion. Nevertheless, being desirous that their names should live as landmarks of excellence to future generations, they besought the prince that he would build two cities, one on the site of each encampment; that on the eastern bank of the river to be called

Zeinabad, (now Jehanabad,) and that on the western bank to be named Boorhanpoor. Hence arose our city.

Ruins of Mohummedan tombs and mosques are thickly scattered through and all around Boorhanpoor; though numbers of these relics of faded grandeur are daily springing up into new life, as the merchant requires a warehouse, or the devotee a cell. Even now, many parts of the city are remarkable for the very elaborate style of its architecture. The streets are wide and regular, and the houses are frequently three, four, or even five, stories in height, which is very unusual in the East. In fashion the houses very much resemble those of Oojein, being built of brick below, and of wood, very richly carved, above; the fronts being tastefully decorated with pillars, cornices, and mouldings of the most intricate designs. The handsomest portions of the city are the Chouk, the Raj Bazaar, and the Burra Bazaar; and the principal buildings of interest are the Jumma Musjid, or chief mosque, the Eed-Ghur, the King's Fort, the palace of the Ahu Kahna, the ruined mosque of Abdool Raheim Kahn, the aqueduct, and some remains of the Madressa.

The Jumma Musjid is the first in importance. It was built at the close of the fifteenth century by Meeran Adil Kahn, a prince of the Farookhi dynasty, and is certainly a credit to the architectural taste of those times. It is built of a fine dark-grey granite, the exterior surface of which, by long exposure to the climate, has assumed a hue fast approaching to black; and this, in conjunction with the majesty of the design, gives the whole pile a tone of solemnity quite overpowering. The plan of the structure is quadrangular, presenting a façade of seventeen arches, which are carried through the body of the building, five deep; and at either extremity is a handsome octagonal minaret. The faces are beautifully carved in arabesque and running border patterns of wreathed flowers; the mouldings are particularly delicate, and are covered in some instances with a profusion of carved tracery; a grand terrace and reservoir occupy the front, and the entire edifice is enclosed within a large court. A circumstance which adds not a little to the mystic effect of the Jumma Musjid, is the extreme nicety with which the blocks of granite are joined; whence it assumes the appearance of having been carved out of one solid block: nothing less than a very close inspection will discover the truth. Another peculiarity is that it is without a single cupola, though these ornaments may be regarded as distinctive of the mosque in all other parts of India. Upon the base of one of the minarets there is an inscription, cut in fine bold Persian characters, of a large size, recording in triumphant terms the conquest of Boorhanpoor and Aseerghur, (in the year A.D. 1599,) by Akbur the

Great, who invaded the kingdom of Bahadoor Kahn, the last monarch of the Farookhi dynasty in Kandeish.

Bahadoor Kahn was a weak and vicious prince, without a redeeming quality to be discovered in his character. In three short years after his succession to a wealthy and powerful kingdom, the reins of government were shaken from his hand, and the glory of the kings of Kandeish was darkened for ever. Immediately upon his accession, he gave himself up to the pleasures and excesses of the seraglio; and, diverting himself with minstrels and dancers, he either neglected altogether the affairs of the state, or amused his evil propensities by adopting all such measures as would tend to loosen the existing restraints upon vice and profligacy among his subjects. So that, in a day, as it were, all morality and social order appeared to have vanished from the kingdom.

The first of Bahadoor Kahn's public misfortunes, and one which materially hastened his downfal, arose from the enmity of Prince Danael Mirza, which he incurred by declining to send the customary congratulations, on his accession to the command of the forces in the Dekkan. Two years subsequently to this impolitic and senseless conduct, the emperor Akbur arrived at Mandao, with the avowed object of invading the unsubdued provinces of the Dekkan; when Bahadoor Kahn, instead of following the wise example of his father by relying upon the honour of Akbur and co-operating with him in his expedition, shut himself up in the fort of Aseer, and prepared himself to withstand the power of the emperor. For this purpose he assembled twenty thousand of his subjects, including all sorts of mechanics and tradespeople within his capital, and also provided himself with immense stores of cattle of every description, as well as of grain and all other necessaries. When Akbur heard of these acts of defiance, he sent orders to his generals-in-chief, Kahn Kahnum and Prince Danael Mirza, to continue the siege of Ahmednuggur, while, in the interval, he himself marched to the south and took possession of Boorhanpoor, and one of his generals laid siege to Aseer. The wonderful resources possessed by Bahadoor Kahn, and the impregnable character of the defences of Aseer, might have enabled that prince, had he possessed even a measure of prudence and energy, to have endured a siege of many years. But, owing to the lazy spirit of the garrison, and the want of attention on the part of the proper authorities, and owing also to the continued season of debauchery which reigned within the fortress, the common duties in every department of the service were altogether neglected; and soon, from the accumulation of filth and the great numbers of cattle which dying daily were suffered to lie where they had fallen, the place became a sink of pollution. Hence, the air being contaminated, a fetid epidemic was engendered, which raged for a length of time, and slew hundreds daily.

At this period, there existed a common belief that the great and successful emperor Akbur assisted himself in the art of war by the practice of necromancy, and the new calamities which daily beset the once proud garrison of Aseer seemed to confirm the vulgar opinion. A report was circulated that a council of magicians accompanied the besieging army; and in consequence of his credulity, Bahadoor Kahn, although he continued to endure the blockade, neglected even the commonest precautions for his safety, alleging that, since his misfortunes arose from the above-mentioned cause, it was not in the power of man to avert them; and that any efforts for that purpose would only tend to increase the accumulation of evil. The dead were suffered to lie in the streets and houses, a prey to birds and vermin; the sick were abandoned to their wretched fate; and the cattle died in thousands from starvation, not from the scarcity of provender, but for want of a hand to feed them.

At this juncture, the besiegers stormed and carried the lower fort, called Mallighur. Nothing could exceed the infatuation of Bahadoor Kahn, who, since the commencement of the siege, appeared to have come suddenly under the influence of extreme avarice; for although he had at this time ten years' store of grain, and treasure to an enormous amount, yet he continued to keep his troops in arrears, and upon the most niggardly supplies of food. They, therefore, seeing no chance of redress, and at length worn out with calamity and terror, resolved to seize upon their prince, and hand him over to the enemy. Before their scheme could be effected, however, it reached the ears of one of Bahadoor Kahn's ladies, who immediately apprised her lord of his danger; and he, having summoned his ministers to a special council, sought their advice as to how he should best avert the threatening danger. The nobles, weakened by long indulgence and debauchery, and dismayed by the melancholy aspect of affairs, felt no disposition to cope with the gathering difficulties; and advised their sovereign that it was then too late to seek a remedy, and that his only safety would be found in submission to the enemy. Bahadoor Kahn immediately opened negotiations for the surrender of the fortress, proudly alleging that the pestilence alone, and not the arms of his enemies, had reduced him to such a necessity. He demanded, in his conditions, that the lives of all his garrison should be spared, and that all personal property should be secured to the owners. Akbur returned for answer, that, as for the lives and property of his followers, if there were any left, they should be held sacred; that the life of Bahadoor Kahn should be given him for repentance; but that, since he was unacquainted with the proper use and value of money, the emperor Akbur would condescend to become his treasurer. The amount of wealth which the conqueror thus considerately took under his care proved to be enormous. It is in commemoration of these events that the Persian inscription above described was carved upon the mosque. The greatness and power of the kings of Kandeish sunk in the ruin of Bahadoor Kahn; but their blood is not extinct; for there is now residing at Boorhanpoor a nobleman of considerable wealth and influence, who is the representative of the family.

Not far from the Jumma Musjid, stands the mosque of Abdool Raheim Kahn, which forms the subject of the accompanying plate, the minarets of the Jumma Musjid being seen in the distance. The body of building is in ruin, and the greater part of the roof has fallen, in consequence of the wooden pillars which supported it having decayed at their bases, or having been eaten away by the white ants. The minarets are peculiarly slender, and scarcely less lofty than those of the Jumma Musjid; but they are sadly neglected, and the weather consequently forces an entrance on all sides. It is, however, reported that the more public-spirited among "the faithful" in Boorhanpoor are talking about repairing the whole edifice.

The Eedghur is a building to be found in almost every Mohummedan town. It consists of a single wall, built with its front facing the east, and is usually ornamented with small minarets and niches;

Drawn by E. Warren, from a sketch by Capt. Meadows Taylor. Engraved by Fisher.

Mosque of Abdool Raheem Kahn, Boorhanpoor.

one niche larger than the rest, in the centre, being used as a pulpit for the chief *moolla*. It is especially dedicated to the mysteries of the Bukra Eed, an annual festival, in commemoration of the trial of Abraham's faith, when commanded by the Almighty to offer his son Isaac as a burnt sacrifice on Mount Moriah. The festival is always very noisy, but some of the ceremonies are peculiarly solemn and imposing, especially that wherein they perform the grand sacrifice of a he-goat.

The Eedghur at Burhanpoor possesses a grandeur of design, and an importance of extent, seldom, perhaps nowhere else, to be met with in these buildings. It is said to have been erected by order of the emperor Aurungzebe, who, happening to arrive at Boorhanpoor on the anniversary of the Bukra Eed, was surprised by inquiring in vain for the Eedghur, until informed that the city of Boorhanpoor, though rich in commerce, and a favourite resort of the mighty, had never yet been able to boast of such an edifice. The emperor expressed his astonishment at the circumstance, and severely animadverted upon the want of religious ardour on the part of the Prophet's followers in this city. At the same time, being desirous of setting them a better example, and of exciting something like religious emulation among them, he gave orders for the building of an Eedghur, which should surpass in size and magnificence all others to be seen in the regions of Hindostan, commanding that no expense should be spared upon the work.

The façade is eight hundred and twenty feet in length, and the minarets are upwards of a hundred feet in height. The entire structure, which is unusually solid, is composed of very small bricks, overlaid with pearl chunam, which rivals white marble in brilliancy of colour and polish. The niches are very deep and are beautifully ornamented, particularly that in the centre. From its position, too, the building assumes additional grandeur, forming a grand and striking object in the landscape, from whatever point it is viewed. Some pious slave of the great prophet has lately expended a large sum in planting the terrace in front of it with young mango trees; and, in their present state, they certainly improve the appearance of the spot, and are interesting tokens of religious zeal; but it is to be hoped, that he who planted them has provided means for checking their growth, or intends to have them continually exchanged, as they emerge from their infancy; otherwise, alas! in the course of a few years, the materials of the Eedghur may as well be appropriated for the building of a resident's mansion, or a new range of barracks; for all that will remain visible will be just enough of the minarets to mark the spot.

In the background of this picture is seen a range of high hills, about four miles distant from the city.

From these heights a rivulet is conducted to the city in a handsome aqueduct, raised upon a series of grotesque columns, in which the Mohummedan and Hindoo styles of architecture are mixed. The water is carried over the country by a series of levels, falling one below the other in unequal lengths, from height to height, until it reaches the plain. This, in a measure, breaks that formality which generally renders an aqueduct an offence to the eye in a landscape scene, rather than an ornament. The bold character of the hills, too, and the expanse of the champaign country through which the building is carried, greatly assist its effect ; and altogether the work exhibits considerable skill and taste on the part of the architect. The supply of water thus brought into the city is abundant, and is distributed through every street, in a manner which keeps it cool, and preserves it from impurities, and which prevents the usual annoyance of the bathing and dabbling of the children wherever water is to be found. It is conveyed through all parts of the city in large tunnels sunk a considerable depth below the pavement, and is drawn up through apertures fitted with a cover, to each of which is appended a small windlass, with a leather bucket, for the common use.

The river Tupti flowing past the city in a clear and beautiful stream, renders all this care and expense for the supply of water an enigma to the stranger; until he has tasted the river water, which is so highly impregnated with nitre as to be quite unfit for domestic purposes. Indeed, the Tupti, although a lovely addition to the beauty of the scene, is utterly useless to the inhabitants of Boorhanpoor; for, besides the unserviceable quality of its waters, it is too shallow for the purposes of navigation, being in most places fordable, and nowhere navigable, even to small boats, for more than a few hundred yards at a reach; except during the monsoon, when a few flat-bottomed ferry-boats may be seen plying up and down and across the stream. It was in the middle of this river that the grand elephant fights used, in days of old, to take place, for the amusement of the royal inhabitants of the palace. Thevenot, who visited the city, about A. D. 1666, describes an extraordinary monument of an elephant, erected in the stream by Shah Jehan; but it has now disappeared. This entertaining author writes thus:—"In the same place there is a figure of an elephant done to the natural bigness; it is of a reddish shining stone; the back parts of it are in the water, and it leans to the left side. The elephant (which that statue represents) died in that place, fighting before Shah Jehan, (the father of Aurungzebe,) who would needs effect a monument to the beast, because he loved it; and the Gentiles besmear it with colours as they do their Pagods."

The palace of the Ahu Kahna stands on the north

bank of the river, commanding a fine view of the country above described; it is a spacious, but not particularly elegant building, the principal interest attached to it arising from its antiquity, its excellent preservation in defiance of neglect and exposure, and the evidence which its design and structure exhibit of the refined luxury of those by whom it was planned. The inhabitants affirm that it was the work of Aurungzebe, but it is plainly of much greater antiquity. Its halls and courts, its baths, reservoirs, fountains, pavilions, and shaded terraces, though disfigured by weather-stains, and polluted by noxious vermin and all sorts of unclean birds and beasts, bear evidence of having been designed with a strict attention to the most extravagant modes of gratifying voluptuousness, and with less regard than usual to unnecessary ornament. The building was probably used as a seraglio, rather than as the court residence; for it is entirely surrounded with a high wall, such as usually encloses only the apartments of the women. A broad space around the walls is planted with pepul and tamarind trees of the most luxuriant growth, and of a venerable antiquity, probably not inferior to that of the building; for both species are of peculiarly slow vegetation, and of great longevity. The fruit gardens, which were very extensive, are now overrun with jungul and rank weeds, of a gigantic stature peculiar to the tropics. Altogether, the scene is one of wild desolation and waste rarely to be equalled, this effect being heightened in no common degree by the substantial though neglected state of the building;

> All tenantless, save to the crannying wind.

The King's Fort is also upon the north bank of the river, and consists of an enormous mass of building, rising pile above pile to the citadel, which crowns the summit. The historian Ferishta affirms that it was built by Meeran Adil Kahn, who came to the throne of Kandeish in A. D. 1457, and was one of the most powerful monarchs of the Farookhi dynasty. The gigantic monument which he has here raised to his own memory, is calculated to endure for ages, yet to come, as a proof of the grandeur of his mind, and of the power and wealth by which he was enabled to display it.

The citadel, though less ponderous than other parts of the fort, is not the least peculiar of its features, being constructed in a succession of massive arcades, towering one above the other to a giddy height, upon the very summit of which the royal founder had raised his seraglio, and probably his own private palace. The several arcades which form the lofty foundation of this seraglio could hardly have been intended for occupation, except, perhaps, for the guards and menials; the interior being laid out in a succession of small, dark apartments, which have more the appearance of dungeons than places of residence. The look-out upon the scenery from this royal perch is truly sublime, extending over an immense expanse of beautifully-undulated country, watered by the Tupti, and commanding a view of all the surrounding towns and villages, for many miles. The lower parts of the fort are abandoned to all the destructive powers of the elements, and the no less formidable, though more subtle, ravages of vegetation ; yet the passage of ages appears to have effected upon these solid structures as little injury as the same number of years would have produced upon the ordinary works of man. This is the more striking, from the circumstance, that nearly all the surrounding buildings,—which, though of a more modern date, are also of a less substantial construction,—are running very rapidly to decay. Their roofs have nearly all fallen ; many of their walls are also prostrate ; and the hand of time lies heavily, both upon their form and material.

One suite of chambers alone is an exception to this remark ; for, although of a light and elegant design, the apartments are still in fine preservation ; at the same time it is probable that they are of a much later period than the rest of the fort. The exterior is not remarkable for beauty, and the entrance is so mean and obscure, so overgrown with weeds and shrubs, as to escape the notice of a passing spectator. Chance, or a minute examination of the building, alone reveals the low archway by which admittance is to be gained. The surprise and gratification of the visitor to the interior are heightened by the unexpected magnificence of the chambers to which he is thus introduced. They are three in number; that in the centre being the most remarkable for extent and the splendour of its decorations. The material is white marble of the finest quality, elaborately carved into tracery and fret-work of endless variety, and of a delicacy equal in design and execution. The roof is supported, or rather formed, by numberless gothic arches, which spring from slender shafts of perfect symmetry, and intersect each other in all directions, terminating in thousands of wreathed flowers, which again are formed into groins and stalactical pendants of wonderful beauty. The flooring is also of white marble, and in the centre of the apartment is a beautiful basin of the same material, from which, in former days, a large jet of water was thrown up almost to the roof, whence it descended in a thick shower, and fell upon an inclined plane running round the interior of the basin: this being cut into shell-shaped hollows, here and there, created a pleasant murmuring sound, calculated to induce drowsiness and repose, luxuries beyond all price to the voluptuous Asiatic. Like most of the other buildings in the fort, this elegant edifice is now utterly deserted, except by certain desolation-loving tenants, supposed by the Hindoos to embody the souls of those who built the place and once resided there in regal splendour.

> 'Tis now the raven's dark abode;
> 'Tis now the apartment of the toad;
> And there the fox securely feeds;
> And there the poisonous adder breeds,
> Concealed in ruins, moss, and weeds.

Near this building stands another, forming the most complete contrast which design could have placed in juxtaposition with it. This is a mosque, or rather the mouldering remains of one, built of black granite. The greater part of it is now prostrate, but the minarets remain firm, being almost as sharp and perfect as at the time of their erection, excepting the cupolas with which they are surmounted: these are much shattered, as if by lightning. The lower part of the fort terminates, on the river side, in a handsome flight of steps leading to the water's edge. Here the scene is varied by a group of Hindoo temples, around which are usually to be seen crowds of Hindoo women, gaily clad, assembling to bathe, or perform their *pooja* (prayer), and passing to and fro with their vari-formed water-pots, piled up one above the other on their heads.

Upon the inland side of the fort, leading directly from the entrance, is the Chouk; adjoining it is the Raj Bazaar, remarkable for the peculiar style of the houses. These are generally fronted with wooden verandas, very richly carved, projecting, at all angles, into the streets, in picturesque confusion, and exhibiting every diversity of form into which anything in the nature of a veranda can be twisted. The accompanying plate, entitled the Suba's house, represents one of the finest specimens of this kind of building to be found in Boorhanpoor. The lower parts only are supported by masonry, the upper stories being built entirely of wood. The carving is extremely bold, and yet beautifully finished, and represents not only fruit and flowers, but various emblematic devices of birds and beasts. The capitals of the pillars, and the bosses, and cornices, are wonderfully elaborate in design, and delicate in execution. The house is about a hundred years old, and was built by a Maharhatta Brahmin, who was at that time Suba, or governor of the city. It is still in the possession of his family, most of whom are wealthy, and hold offices under Sihndia's government. It is situate at the head of the Raj Bazaar, a broad handsome street, formed by rows of houses, much in the same style of architecture, though somewhat inferior in size and beauty. These are the residences of the principal merchants, who, in the days of Boorhanpoor's commercial glory, were notorious, thoughout India, for their great wealth and power. Now, the richest among them are inferior in this respect to those of Delhi and Benares, many of whom, complaining bitterly of poverty and poverty's hard fare, are rolling in secret wealth, and living

Drawn by C. Bibden from a Sketch by Capt. Meadows Taylor. Engraved by J. B. Varrall.

The Subas House, Boorhanpoora.

London, Published Oct. 1, 1839, by Charles Tilt, 86, Fleet Street.

in humble homes, mere sheds compared with those here spoken of. The bazaars are, perhaps, the most entertaining resort for the visitor, in all Oriental cities; but in Boorhanpoor they are especially so, as much on account of the intelligence and civility of the merchants, as by reason of the brilliant articles exposed for sale, and the handsome but peculiar style of the buildings.

Here, these public places of business are certainly as full of noise and bustle as are all other similar places in India; that is to say, they are as full of noise and bustle as the very essence of noise and bustle can possibly render them. Hither, in the cool of the evening, the merchants of all tribes, of all degrees, and of every trade, throng, for the purposes of traffic; and hither, likewise, resort the idlers and the gossips, no less in number than the men of business. The more substantial traders occupy small shops, or warehouses, in front of which is a narrow open veranda, where the proprietor is seated, or reclines upon a mat with a comfortable cushion, and is usually to be seen smoking his *hookka* or *kulliàn*. Between each lengthened whiff he engages in earnest treaty with a brother merchant; making his salaams to all his acquaintance as they pass; at times, he gives directions to his slave within the shop; listens to his book-keeper, who reads over the account of his day's barter; or, perchance, if he be a devout disciple of the Prophet, with spectacles stuck on the extreme tip of his nose, and retained there, after the native fashion, by a string passed behind the ears, his Khoran spread carefully upon his crossed legs, his face towards Mekka, he reads, for his own benefit, in a sing-song voice, audible to all passengers—whom, by way of episode, he, from time to time, congratulates with a *salaam aleikoom*, or a scrap of the latest news. When a customer offers himself, he is not admitted within the shop, as in Europe, but the merchant calls for the required goods, one article only being produced at a time, and changed again and again until of the required kind or quality. These men are chiefly traders in brocades, muslins, bullion, cloth of gold, shawls, arms, and jewels. The petty dealers and pedlers have, as is meet, a more humble way of doing business; for they have usually no shop, and all their wares are arranged upon the bare ground, or upon a carpet spread before them.

Some years since, the trade of Boorhanpoor was unrivalled in the Dekkan. The immense demand upon its market, occasioned by the quartering of the Maharhatta armies round about it, and the consumption in the courts of Sihndia, of Holkur, of the Rajas of Sathara and Guikawa, made princes of its former merchants, and drew thither speculators from all regions of the East.

The chief article of manufacture is the *kullabuttoo*, or gold and silver thread, used in the weaving of muslins, brocades, &c. It is said to be very superior to that of any other place in India, and the process by which it is made appears to be peculiar, though very simple. A short description may be interesting. A piece of the purest silver is beaten into a cylindrical form, about the size of a man's finger; after this is done, the metal is beaten out with hammers to a considerable length, that is, until it can be passed through an orifice about the eighth of an inch in diameter. It is then drawn through a successive series of perforations in a plate of hard metal, decreasing in size until it is reduced to the fineness of a common bobbin thread. In this state it is wound upon several small reels, which work upon steel pivots, in a bench constructed for the purpose; the ends of the threads are again passed through still smaller holes, in a similar plate to the former, and are then affixed to a large reel, which, being set rapidly in motion, draws the wire finer and finer by each repeated operation, until it is reduced to the required size. When this is accomplished, it is passed to another set of workmen, to be flattened; a part of the process requiring great dexterity. The threads being wound upon small reels, as at first, are taken, five at a time, in the hand of the workman, who draws them gradually over a small anvil of highly polished steel, hitting them smartly and rapidly with a small square hammer, as they are moved. It is evident that the greatest nicety is required in regulating the weight and the time of the blow, so that the metal may be wrought to an exact equality of breadth and thickness. This done, it is handed over to be plated, upon silk, by another set of workmen, whose sleight of hand must be still more perfect than that of the former. The silk thread being chosen exactly to accord with the breadth of the metal, is passed over a small pulley, attached to the ceiling of the room; it is then fastened to a spindle with a long crank, which is kept in rapid motion by an occasional kick from the workman, who, having the metal coiled up on the floor behind him, affixes it to the silk, and guides it with such consummate skill, as precisely to cover the thread without flaw or inequality. Not the least wonderful part of this juggling craft appears to be, that for the purpose of obtaining a gold thread it is only necessary to gild the lump of silver, as a first process, before it is drawn into wire, after which it will retain its gilding, as though it were a solid lump of gold, through all the beatings and drawings and windings which are bestowed upon it, until the thread is perfected.

The proprietors of these gold-thread manufactories are, for the most part, a peculiar sect of Mohummedans known by the name of Bohra, but styling themselves by the prouder title of Ishmaela. They occupy about five hundred of the best houses in the city, and are in every sense respectable, being the most wealthy of the commercial classes, and having the repute of liberal and fair dealers. They are, moreover, scrupulously observant of their religious duties, and daily attend their mosque, nearly two miles distant from the city, although they are not under the immediate surveillance of their *moolla*, or chief priest; whose custom it is to reside at Surat, paying his flock at Boorhanpoor an annual visit to collect his dues and leave his blessing. In appearance these Bohras strongly resemble the Arabs, their features and complexions being of the Arabian cast, as well as the fashion of their garments; and it is probable that they are really of Arabian origin, though they have been many centuries resident in the Dekkan and in Guzerat.

NASSUK.

The Hindoo inhabitants of Nassuk relate a great diversity of tales, some Brahminical, and some Budhistical, descriptive of the origin of their city. The Mussulmans also claim the distinction of having been its founders; and as they have but one story concerning it, and that a particularly picturesque one, while it is likewise the most probable, I shall venture to translate it. They affirm that its foundation was the work of a very notorious character in the Mogul history, one

YAKOOB LAIS, THE BANDIT CHIEF,

who afterwards raised himself to be governor of the province of Sehistan. The legend is thus told:—

About the middle of the ninth century in the Christian era, when Dherm-ben-Nassuk was governor of the province of Sehistan, there lived in the city of Herat one Lais-ul-Suffar, a brazier, who had three sons, Yakoob, Omar, and Ali, youths remarkable for their manly beauty, their undaunted courage, and

Drawn by C. Bibden from a sketch by Capt. Meadows Taylor. Engraved by J. Smith.

Nassuk, on the Guadavery.

London Published Oct 1, 1839, by Charles Tilt 86 Fleet Street.

great personal strength and activity. According to Oriental custom, they were educated to the trade of their forefathers; but Yakoob, the eldest, being of a proud ambitious disposition, and filled with the spirit of adventure, was no sooner free from the bondage of his apprenticeship, than he cast aside the tools of his humble calling, and with them the designation *ul-Suffar* (the brazier); assuming the sabre and shield, as implements more in accordance with his taste than the hammer and anvil. Having enlisted under the banners of Mohummed Tahir, he soon discovered that the subordination of a soldier's life was even less tolerable than that which he had quitted; but at the same time, being delighted with the excitement of strife and the prospect of military plunder, he determined to wage war upon his own account.

The bent of Yakoob Lais's mind had led him to associate with the most daring *pulwans* (athletes) among his comrades, men whose prowess and courage were unrivalled; but who, in one respect unlike himself, having been bred to arms and the discipline of a soldier's life from childhood, felt not the hardship of restraint. Laying before these men the temptations of booty and enterprise, he easily induced them to join him upon certain secret predatory excursions, in which he acted as their leader; and so large were their emoluments, so fascinating their adventures, that he had ultimately little difficulty in persuading them to desert from the army, and give themselves up wholly to a life of plunder. He thus gained the command of about fifty bold and hardy veterans, who, confident in the skill and undaunted spirit of their young, yet circumspect captain, and charmed by his hearty good-humour, no less than they were astonished at his wit and superior understanding, pledged themselves by exchange of turbans, and swore on their swords to make his will their only law.

Yakoob Lais and his formidable troop for a while established themselves in the rocky fastnesses upon the southern frontier of Sehistan, and levied contributions, not only upon all travellers, but also upon all towns and villages within the range of a forced march. But, upon one occasion, having penetrated southward as far as the romantic river Guadavery, they brought upon themselves the formidable enmity of the Brahmins in all the country roundabout, by pillaging some Hindoo temples, and carrying off a vast amount of treasure. Being surrounded on all sides, they would, doubtless, have perished, had they not been led by one of their comrades, a native of the place, to a retreat of great security, within the chain of the Western Ghat mountains. The strength and secrecy of this position appear to have been incomparable; and Yakoob Lais, considering it to be admirably adapted to the permanent security of his troop, and the depositing of his treasure, immediately ordered his head-quarters to be removed thither. There was an extensive valley shut in on all sides by bold precipitous rocks, to be entered only by one pass, and that so narrow and intricate, as to be quite impracticable to all, except those who, by long practice, had become thoroughly acquainted with its labyrinthine circuities. A dense forest, rendered impenetrable by thorny underwood, covered the face of this valley on all sides, except upon a spot in the centre, where was a high conical hill,—excavated by the Budhists in former ages—the upper part whereof had been hewn into an immense temple, and the base into numerous caverns for the abodes of the priests. So vast were the proportions of the temple, that it was esteemed capable of containing five hundred mounted troopers. It had two small arched entrances, one towards the east and the other towards the west, protected by huge massive doors of wrought iron; the approach to which was by two circular roads, in the nature of military ramps, which wound round from the base of the hill and rendered the ascent easy for cavalry. The height of this extraordinary chamber was about fifty feet to the centre of the vault. The rocky walls were all around hewn into bassirilievi of gigantic figures, representing the wonderful characters of the Budhistical pantheon, and a multitude of incomprehensible monsters, whose hideous aspects and antic attitudes greatly enhanced the wild and mystic effect of the place. The natural fortification of this position was so perfect, that Yakoob Lais had little to do in preparing it for the accommodation and security of his band. He cut an aperture through the summit of the hill, to admit light and a free circulation of air into the great chamber, and some secret galleries, from apparently inaccessible spots, to communicate with caverns which were to serve as treasuries. He also erected hidden stockades, at intervals, along the pass; so that a handful of men might have defended it effectually against the largest army.

The free and adventurous occupation upon which he had entered was, in every respect, exactly suited to the wild spirit of the daring Yakoob Lais; except only that it appeared to set a limit to his ambition; which suffered him not to regard it as a fixed mode of life, but as a means of obtaining that wealth which he intended should eventually raise him to extended power and importance; and he always encouraged his followers to anticipate a similar improvement in their condition. In this lawless career he found it necessary to exact from his followers, with a firm hand, the most implicit observance of his orders; and, having his future plans always in view, he was especially careful to avoid all cruelty or unnecessary outrage. With so much moderation, indeed, did he practise his misdeeds, that he was never known to pillage the needy, or to deprive any travellers of the whole of their property; but having ascertained their circumstances, he invariably took from them just as much as he thought they might spare, without actually distressing them. At the same time his demeanour was mild and courteous, and his gallantry to females such as had gained him the admiration of all the fair ones who had been fortunate enough to bestow their jewels and valuables upon him. He omitted no opportunity of increasing the strength of his band, whenever he could do so, with such materials as his very nice discretion might select; until, in the course of time, his force amounted to five hundred gallant horsemen, splendidly appointed, and mounted upon the noblest Persian chargers.

Dherm-ben-Nassuk had frequently heard of the extraordinary exploits of Yakoob Lais, and the other deserters from his army, and had, upon several occasions, sent out expeditions against them; but had never, in any case, been able to cut them off, or discover their retreat; indeed all his detachments had suffered more or less despoliation at the hands of these renowned marauders, without effecting any kind of good. At length, however, having received complaints from all quarters of very extensive robberies, he determined upon taking more active measures for the suppression of the evil, and ordered out a body of three hundred chosen cavalry, whom he, being ignorant of the increased strength of the bandit's gang, supposed would easily destroy, or take them prisoners. The watchful captain, having received information of this impending scheme, immediately wrote a letter of remonstrance to his former chief;

assuring him that he had ever retained a sincere respect for the very name of Dherm-ben-Nassuk, and had quitted the service from no personal dissatisfaction, but solely in consequence of his natural aversion to any form of servitude. He entreated, at the same time, that the threatened expedition might be countermanded; inasmuch as he was most reluctant to engage in a conflict with those, among whom there would necessarily be a number of his former compatriots and boon-companions; and he concluded his letter by assuring Dherm-ben-Nassuk that ten times the strength of the intended detachment would never be able to effect his subjection. In this earnest representation Dherm-ben-Nassuk saw nothing but what he believed to be a cunning attempt to avert impending punishment, and he therefore delivered to Yakoob Lais's messenger, as his only reply, a naked sword, snapped in twain near the hilt; signifying, that no quarter should be given, even though his own party should perish in the attack. So confident was he of success, against a band whom he believed to be not one-sixth part so numerous as his own, that he gave his officer orders to employ only half his force, if that should be found sufficient, and to send the remainder through the country to procure carriage for the transport of the treasure, which, he doubted not, would be very great. At the same time he gave him strict injunctions not to return without the heads of those against whom the expedition was directed.

When the messenger delivered to Yakoob Lais the broken sword sent by Dherm-ben-Nassuk, the purport of the reply was immediately understood by all present, and naturally excited great anger and indignation. The captain, however, coolly took the broken weapon from the bearer, and, handing it to one of the armourers, ordered him to re-set the blade in the hilt; declaring, that although the short-sightedness of Dherm-ben-Nassuk had only enabled him to anticipate one interpretation of the message, he himself could read in it a second, and the true solution:—"For," said he, "the tyrant having by his own act broken his own power, has cast it into my hands, that I might repair and wield it for my own advantage, and that of my trusty followers. Yet, for the sake of those with whom I have broken the bread of friendship, I will, as long as is consistent with our safety, employ the shield of defence, rather than the sword of revenge; even though our enemy is the aggressor, and one who has wantonly threatened us with a cruel extermination." Little, indeed, as the bandit chief had expected so irritating a reply to his pacific remonstrance, his habitual caution had already devised and matured a plan of operations against such an event; but as a part of his general policy was never to divulge his schemes beyond the senior officers, who formed his council of war, he contented himself with assuring the band that he was fully prepared for the worst, and hoped to give Dherm-ben-Nassuk so severe a chastisement for his insolence, as should effectually protect them from all future molestation; and this without so much as drawing a sword against any one of his people. The troops of Yakóob Lais, who had been accustomed to rely with implicit confidence upon the skill of their commander, and to execute all his orders without inquiry as to their purport, were, nevertheless, amazed at his forbearance, and wondered not a little how he would possibly accomplish his extraordinary purpose; at the same time they were greatly amused by the singularity of the design, and anxious to show their willing obedience.

Yakoob Lais now called to his presence Aboo Dudmaun, a wily ingenious old fellow, whom he usually employed as a spy in cases of emergency. He ordered him to disguise himself as a Mohummedan *fakhir*, and to throw himself in the way of Dherm-ben-Nassuk's troops; and when questioned, as would be probable, for information concerning the banditti, to heap unmeasured reproach and abuse upon them. This behaviour would, of course, instigate his examiners to press for information, when his part would be to confess, with apparent reluctance, that he had been, until lately, their priest; that having acquired a large sum of money by his religious services, which it had been his intention to devote to the foundation of a sanctuary, he had been basely plundered by command of Yakoob Lais, and turned adrift upon the world. He was, throughout, to exhibit such a spirit of wrath and revenge, as would suggest to the party the possibility of gaining his services; and at last he should suffer himself to be induced, by a rich bribe, to betray the retreat of his comrades. His further instructions were to represent the gang as one hundred and fifty strong, and the difficulties so great as to require the entire force of three hundred for their subjection. At the same time he was to conduct them to the cave with sanguine hopes of success, and to heighten their confidence by certain pretended omens and visions.

Other spies besides Aboo Dudmaun were sent out to watch the approach, and to gather news concerning the enemy, and, in a few days, they were reported to be advancing in the direction of the defile leading to the cave. Yakoob Lais immediately put himself at the head of one hundred of his men, having ordered the remainder to secrete themselves in the forest, and to await patiently for his return and further orders. He then marched out upon the plain, and drew up his detachment in battle array, as if awaiting the attack of his enemy, immediately in front of the pass. Meanwhile Dherm-ben-Nassuk's force appeared and continued to advance, until Yakoob Lais could plainly distinguish the person of Aboo Dudmaun. He then sent forth a messenger, with a flag of truce, to demand the person of the traitor *fakhir*, offering the price of a lahk of rupees for his head; but, as he expected, the courier returned unsuccessful; and at his heels, in two close columns, the foe came quickly on, preparing to wheel and charge the bandit's inferior line, on either flank.

At this moment Yakoob Lais rode to the left wing, a little in advance of the line, and was apparently animating his men to stand firm, while, in truth, he was repeating certain secret instructions previously given. The enemy were within five hundred yards. The bandit's line was seen to waver, and, despite his loud and energetic appeals to their courage, the centre soon gave way and fled; the right wing followed them; but a small subdivision of picked men, upon the extreme left, stood fast, until ordered by their commander to retire within the defile. This they did deliberately and in perfect order; and no sooner were they clear of the entrance of the narrow avenue, than a large tree fell prostrate across the pass, effectually intercepting the impetuous career of the assailants, and giving the dispersed freebooters time to rally and beat an orderly retreat.

Having cleared the temporary impediment which had been so suddenly and unexpectedly cast in their path, Dherm-ben-Nassuk's cavalry renewed the pursuit, directed by the false *fakhir*, who displayed a military ardour, and a perfection of horsemanship, which nothing but his late alliance with inborn soldiery could account for. The Dherm-ben-Nassukites, however, considered themselves especially fortunate, in having fallen in with so active and zealous a guide, through such wild and intricate passes; and they followed him with perfect confidence. Here and there they caught a glimpse of the retreating banditti, winding down the rugged water-course in the gorge of a narrow valley, or round the jutting angle of a distant hill, until they entered the forest, where all was deep obscurity. Aboo Dudmaun led them on, continually cautioning them against ambuscades, but expressing a firm conviction that the gang would eventually retire within their principal fastness, for the purpose of defending their treasure; and he, moreover, promised them an easy conquest and immense booty.

Having traversed about three miles of dense forest, the soil whereof was damp, and the air chill, despite the blistering intensity of a tropical sun which blazed upon the foliage above, the pursuing party emerged upon the little *glacis* which surrounded the excavated hill, just in time to behold the rear of the bandit's troop filing up the ramp, and retiring within the eastern entrance to the great cave. Requesting the leader to call a halt, Aboo Dudmaun now suggested that the trunk of some young tree would supply them with such a battering-ram as might be easily wielded by a score of dismounted troopers, and which would enable them to demolish the gates of the cavern by half-a-dozen well-directed blows. The advice was no sooner given than acted upon; and, in less than half an hour, the confident assailants mounted the road to the eastern gate, and applied their newly-made engine to the iron door. The vaulted chamber resounded loudly with the blow, and the rattling and confused clatter of cavalry in motion, was immediately heard within. Another and another blow succeeded, and the massive doors rolled back as if by magic, leaving to them a clear undisputed passage to the interior. Three or four troopers, the tail, as it were, of the flying banditti, dashed hastily through the opposite gate, which immediately closed behind them with a terrible report, awaking a thousand thunders from the rocky sides and roof, which echoed and re-echoed round, till the very foundations of the vaulted chamber trembled sensibly. The startled soldiers who had entered soon regained their confidence, and advanced to the second door, which they found so firmly closed, that their utmost manual efforts could not move or even shake it; yet neither bolt nor bar was visible. They speedily applied the battering-ram, expecting, no doubt, as little resistance as before; but they dealt stroke after stroke with increased force, without producing any effect, except the effect of a very great noise, for the successive blows rang through the vaulted chamber, in a confusion of multiplied vibrations almost deafening.

During the delay caused by this obstruction, the whole body of Dherm-ben-Nassuk's force had filed into the cave; and all, except those who were immediately employed in endeavouring to force the gate, were gazing about in astonishment at the vastness of the place, and the singularity of its decorations—when, suddenly, another report as loud as the first which had been heard, made every heart beat high with apprehension, and sent the affrighted horses plunging and rearing in all directions. The door by which they had entered had closed behind them, and now, like the other, defied their most strenuous exertions to re-open it. After wearying their strength and tempers by repeated, but still ineffectual, efforts, they at last bethought them of their guide, the venerable *fakhir*, and wondered that he had not volunteered his services to extricate them from their dilemma. But they sought him in vain; he was not among them. They saw immediately that they were betrayed, and cursed their own incaution and credulity. The whole scheme of the bandit chief was so plainly laid out before their opened eyes, that they denounced themselves, again and again, as three hundred of the most blind, insensate asses, who could possibly by unpardonable, almost voluntary, negligence, have sacrificed themselves to the clumsy, ill-concealed pitfall of a stupid wolf. Every mesh of the unartful net had been conspicuously laid in their path; they had seen every noose of the snare; and still, in fatal absence of mind, had planted their feet in it. Yet, truly, hath it ever been that

Borne on the evil breeze of Indiscretion,
Mischance blights the ripest fruit of Joy ;
Disgusted at the heedless conduct of Folly,
Fickle Fortune closes the gate of Prosperity.
Patience and Circumspection are the jealous distributors of honour.

When Yakoob Lais had given his captive antagonists an opportunity of ruminating, for a while, upon the bitters of mortification and self-reproach, he mounted to the top of the hill, and discovering himself at the aperture, assured them of their personal safety and of hospitable treatment: "I am convinced," said he sarcastically, "that there can be among you none of my former comrades with whom I have exchanged turbans; for how can a true soldier be false to his honour, under so solemn an obligation? Yet, as I behold in your ranks at least a hundred countenances which are wonderfully familiar to me, I can only conclude that most of you are relations of my former friends. For their sake, then, I shall entertain you honourably, as guests, not as prisoners; and, for this purpose, I have commanded my cooks to prepare for you a sumptuous banquet. Lest, however, there should be any of you whose march has not fully prepared him an appetite, I have provided that your feast shall continue a whole week; and be assured that I have that confidence in your honour, that on the seventh day, when you have all broken my bread and tasted my salt, I shall not hesitate to release you. In the interim, I shall pay a visit to him that sent you, and endeavour to convince him of the injustice of his conduct towards me. If I fail in this object, I shall dismiss him to another region, where his odious want of good principle will render him doubly welcome, and I shall myself endeavour more worthily to fill his place. If I succeed, I shall content myself by drawing from his treasury such an amount as I may deem to be a fair remuneration for my invaluable services." Yakoob Lais concluded his speech by desiring the captives to make themselves perfectly at ease, during his absence, and to demand in his name everything which they might require,—assuring them that they were surrounded by five thousand armed warriors and ten thousand slaves; and that everything which they might desire, except liberty, would be let down to them through the aperture.

The bandit chief having thus far conducted his project with complete success, had yet the most difficult part of it to accomplish; for Dherm-ben-Nassuk dwelt in a strongly fortified palace, well guarded by day and night, and only went out from it upon great public occasions. Yakoob, however, apprehended neither difficulty nor danger, for his plots had never yet been met by defeat or disappointment. Having habited himself in the travelling costume of a Mogul nobleman, he set forward with about fifty followers, ten only of whom appeared armed. He travelled with the speed of a whirlwind; and on the evening of the third day, a little before the time of sunset prayer, he took up his abode for the night in a spacious *moohkburra*, the tomb of a Mohummedan saint, which stood immediately without the walls of Dherm-ben-Nassuk's palace. Immediately upon his arrival, he set ten men, expert sappers and miners, to work within the tomb, to excavate a passage into the palace court. This they had completely performed by midnight, and came to the surface in one of the chambers of the treasury. Taking with him only ten of his followers, he entered the palace, all the interior doors whereof, according to Eastern custom, were wide open; and slaves lay asleep upon the floors, in all the passages, with their swords and spears beside them. In profound silence, and with the stealthy movements of a cat, he, as a precautionary measure, first gathered up all the arms, and sent them to the tomb. Then, having collected all the most precious of the costly things which lay around, consisting of various small articles of furniture of pure gold inlaid with gems, and several caskets of court jewels and regalia of inestimable value, including the Mogul cap of state, (the weight of the princely jewels therein being six *seers**) he had them speedily packed up into convenient bales, and ordered them to be removed to the tomb; where his horse was already prepared, his troopers in

* About twelve pounds weight.

their saddles awaiting his return, and ready to start at a moment's notice.

Yakoob Lais was then about to seek out Dherm-ben-Nassuk, for the purpose of extorting from him some oath or bond of impunity, which might protect him from future aggression, and to demand from him certain other advantages which he had resolved to obtain, or otherwise to assassinate him. He was in the act of turning from his followers to execute his purpose, when he struck his foot against some small thing, which went rattling along the polished pavement, and he observed it to sparkle. Thinking that nothing less than diamonds could have reflected light in such a dark place, he picked it up, and not knowing exactly what to make of it, he put it to his tongue. That little act, insignificant as it may appear, caused the immediate subversion of all his schemes, even at the moment of their complete accomplishment. Yakoob Lais had tasted the salt of Dherm-ben-Nassuk; for the supposed jewel was in truth no other than a little lump of rock-salt. Though mortified and disappointed beyond description, his avarice and revenge instantly gave way before his respect for what he esteemed to be an infrangible law of honour and hospitality. He commanded his men to restore everything which had been carried away; and having piled the bales of treasure and bundles of arms in a heap, he wrote in large characters upon the marble wall, with the point of his dagger, "YAKOOB LAIS." He then withdrew, and returned to his head-quarters with all possible speed. Having arrived there on the evening of the sixth day, he held an audience of his whole band, and informed them of the singular circumstance by which the object of his excursion had been defeated; taking the opportunity of urging upon them, as was his constant practice, his favourite maxim,—that among soldiers a nice sense of honour was more estimable than success, and an irreproachable conscience more precious than heaps of treasure. Having explained to them all which had occurred since his departure, he next informed them that, upon his journey homeward, he had planned a manœuvre, which he intended to put in execution the following morning, and by which he yet hoped to impress upon the mind of Dherm-ben-Nassuk such a notion of their strength and power, as would effectually preserve them from all future molestation.

Soon after the dawn of the seventh day from that on which the soldiers of Dherm-ben-Nassuk had been imprisoned, they were again addressed by Yakoob Lais, from the aperture in their prison's roof. Having inquired in friendly terms for their welfare, and expressed a hope that they and their horses had been provided with all that they could want, the generous bandit then told them openly the whole history of his excursion to their master's palace, and assured them that, in accordance with his promise, he was then about to set them at liberty. When he had done speaking, the western door,—that by which the captives had entered,—rolled back upon its massive hinges, and they beheld the narrow *meidan* round about the foot of the hill thronged with cavalry leisurely passing to and fro; while, here and there, through openings in the forest, were seen numbers of single horsemen dispersed about in all directions; so that it was impossible to form any conception of their real strength. In obedience to Yakoob Lais's command, Dherm-ben-Nassuk's troops formed three deep, and marched out of their prison with their sabres drawn. They had much ado, however, to keep their order, owing to the narrowness of the road; and the less expert, as well as those with intractable horses, were fain to ride two deep. They were, however, warmly cheered and greeted on all sides by the banditti, to whom they replied with an honest assurance of friendship; and when they had all marched out upon the plain, Yakoob formed them in line, facing the hill, and requested that they would see his troops pass in review, in order that they might carry a true report to Dherm-ben-Nassuk, concerning their training and appointment. Presently a body of Yakoob Lais's most magnificently caparisoned horsemen, in column four deep, were seen galloping up the winding road leading to the eastern entrance of the great cavern; and in a few seconds they came dashing headlong, at an equal pace and with unbroken order, through the western portal, and continued their apparently perilous career until they reached the plain again, where they dispersed and leisurely entered the forest. Fifty squadrons, each one hundred strong, thus passed in review before the astonished Dherm-ben-Nassukites, who expressed their admiration by continued shouts of applause. When the last squadron had disappeared, the chief expressed his regret that he was unable to exhibit to his guests the wonderful feats of arms and horsemanship which were the daily practice of a certain picked division of his troops, one thousand in number, who were then absent upon a distant expedition. Then having distributed *pawn* to the officers, as a mark of honourable dismissal, he furnished them with a guard of honour to conduct them through the pass, and bade them take their leave.

Meanwhile the greatest anxiety prevailed at the court of Dherm-ben-Nassuk concerning the fate of the detachment, of whom not one word of news had been received, since they had entered the pass in pursuit of the banditti. The greatest apprehension was excited by the circumstance of Yakoob Lais's visit to the palace: for on the morning after that event, the mystery which attached to the position of things upon the first discovery was sufficiently cleared up by the salt, which was found scattered about the floor, where Yakoob Lais had thrown it down, and by the writing upon the wall. In truth, a very accurate surmise was made as to all the facts relating to the occurrence; but, at the same time, it gave rise to a thousand fears for the fate of the three hundred gallant horsemen who had been sent out against the marauders. When, therefore, after seven or eight days of apprehension and suspense, they all returned in safety to their quarters, they were received with surprise and delight; and the relation of their extraordinary adventures excited in Dherm-ben-Nassuk, and all who heard it, the greatest admiration of the bandit chief, especially when they were told of the great strength and wonderful discipline of his followers. Dherm-ben-Nassuk immediately made a vow of inviolable amity towards him, expressing an impatience to exchange turbans with him, and thus secure his friendship and valuable alliance. So greatly was he captivated by the robber's generosity, his skill, and his nice sense of honour, that he ultimately despatched an embassy, inviting him to court, and offering him a high title of nobility, and the command of ten thousand horse. Upon receipt of this message, Yakoob Lais was as much surprised as he was delighted by so magnificent a proposal; and seeing therein a shadow of still grander prospects, he immediately expressed his readiness to accept it, provided only that a knowledge of the truth, as to the number of his followers, should make no alteration in Dherm-ben-Nassuk's desire for his services. He then explained that his little corps of five hundred men had been magnified into a force of ten times its real strength, by reassembling within the forest as soon as they had broken off, and mounting the hill again, upon the opposite side; so that they might as easily have been made to assume the appearance of a hundred thousand. This circumstance, being reported to Dherm-ben-Nassuk, by no means diminished his favour towards Yakoob Lais; on the contrary, he replied that the ingenuity displayed by the manœuvre was well worth ten thousand men, even of such choice troops as were those of the bandit.

Yakoob Lais was forthwith raised to the title of Nawab, and promoted to the command of ten thousand cavalry. He soon afterwards became commander-in-chief, and ultimately, upon the death of Dherm-ben-Nassuk, realized all his dreams of glory, by succeeding to the government of Sehistan. He reigned in absolute sovereignty for a period of eleven years; and has left among the historians of that time a character distinguished for acute intelligence, for undaunted courage, for moderation and temperance, for inflexible justice, and for unbounded generosity. Having greatly extended the dominion of his predecessor, by a career of active enterprise, and the extraordinary success which attended all his undertakings, one of his last acts was, to lay the foundation of a city upon the bank of the river Guadavery, on the very spot where he had formerly pillaged the Brahminical temples; and he called the place Nassuk, to commemorate the name of his late chief and benefactor. For the same purpose, he gave to the cavernous stronghold, which had been for so long a period the favourite head-quarters of his band, the imposing name of Dherm-Raj-Lena.

Moslem influence has now altogether disappeared from the city of Nassuk, and it has become the chief seat and centre of Brahminical learning and religious fraud in the west of India. It is densely populated; nearly forty thousand inhabitants being crowded into a space not exceeding four miles in circuit. Of these, only one hundredth part are Mussulmans; and the remains of Mussulman buildings are quite as scarce, in proportion to the multitude of Hindoo structures. The temples are well nigh innumerable, and many of them remarkably picturesque; they appear, indeed, to have been erected for the purpose of exemplifying the almost infinite diversity of form of which the vaulted roof is susceptible. The hill and Budhistical excavations of Dherm-Raj-Lena are still to be seen, about six miles distant from the city.

The river Guadavery, which enjoys a fame for sanctity scarcely inferior to that of the Ganges, is here but a little brook. Opposite the city the bed has been built up to a succession of levels, so as to form a number of reservoirs, through which the stream flows, and falls from one to the other in a series of cascades. The sources of this river are in the Western Ghàt mountains, whence it issues in innumerable rivulets, many of which are considerably larger than that to which the Hindoos, without any apparent reason, have assigned the honour of pre-eminence. The waters which thus rise to the surface within fifty miles of the Western Ocean, flow eastward, and having formed a junction just above the town of Koombharri, roll on, eastward and south-eastward, through stupendous forests of the *teak*-tree, being joined by numerous other currents, and performing altogether a course of nearly a thousand miles, until it pours itself into the Eastern Ocean, dividing the coasts of Coromandel and Orissa. After the heavy rains, particularly during the monsoon, the volume of its waters is stupendous. Its channel is singularly irregular, being in some places spread over a tract of country two or three miles in breadth, the stream being scarcely knee-deep; while in other parts it is pent up in a narrow bed, the overhanging banks whereof are scarcely a furlong apart, and the waters from eighty to a hundred feet in depth. The most remarkable instance of this kind is at the famous pass through the Papkoondur mountains, which form the north-west frontier of Rajamundri, where the broad current is suddenly compressed into a narrow channel, about two hundred yards in width, by a natural barrier, some parts of which have an altitude exceeding two thousand feet.

HYDRABAD AND BIDUR.

THERE are in Hindostan two large cities, called Hydrabad. One, the capital of the principality of Sihnd, which is situated upon a devious branch of the river Indus, about three miles distant from the main channel; and the other, the capital of the Nizam's dominions, standing on the banks of the Moosa, in the southern quarter of the Dekkan. The latter forms the subject of the present sketch.

The celebrated fortress of Golkonda was, during many generations, the capital of these provinces; but that enterprising prince, Mohummed Kooli Kootab Shah, determined to escape its many incurable inconveniences, by removing the seat of government to a more favoured spot. He had no occasion to wander far in quest of a convenient site, and he ultimately built a city, about six miles south-east from Golkonda, upon the south bank of the river Moosa. This occurred A.D. 1585; and, when the city was complete, the royal founder named it Bhàgnuggur in honour of his favourite mistress Bhàgmutti; but after the death of this lady, the romantic name Bhàgnuggur, which also signifies "Garden Residence," was changed to Hydrabad. The presence of the court speedily secured to the new city a flourishing commercial population; and the nobles vied with each other in the magnificence of their palaces and gardens. The prince also founded several elegant mosques, schools, hospitals, baths, and other public buildings, including a bridge over the Moosa, and set apart a large fund for their maintenance.

The most splendid of those erections is the Char Minar (four minarets), a beautiful quadrangular mosque raised upon four gateways and standing in the centre of the city, so as to open upon each of the four principal streets by a gigantic archway. From the angles of the base spring four stupendous minarets, two hundred and twenty feet in height, and of great solidity. The gateways are covered in by a shallow dome, upon which a superstructure is raised, forming a commodious mosque, with its reservoir of water, all handsomely decorated with Saracenic sculpture. In the quadrangle below there is also a large basin of water, from the centre whereof, on grand occasions, a copious fountain throws up a spout of water almost to the vaulted roof, which falling on all sides in a thick shower, creates a refreshing coolness, highly attractive to thes treet-loungers and gossips. In each of the minarets are apartments appropriated to the use of the professors and students of the college; facetiously said, by Farishta, to have been allotted to them that they might be enabled to look down upon the pomp and

Drawn by H. Warren from a Sketch by Capt. Meadows Taylor — Engraved by J. Redaway

The Char Minar, Hyderabad.

London. Published Oct. 1. 1839 by Charles Tilt 86 Fleet Street.

wealth of this world, and behold in them nothing but insignificance.

The city continued to flourish and to enjoy peace for several years after its foundation; Mohummed Kooli Kootab Shah devoting his energies to the advancement of civilization, and the improvement of the laws. But at length, cupidity having gained access to his heart, he resolved upon undertaking a campaign, for the purpose of extending his territories. His first aim was to possess himself, if possible, of the diamond mines at Moosa-ul-moroo, and he accordingly made a vigorous attack upon that place; but was repulsed with great loss. He ultimately succeeded, however; and likewise reduced all the neighbouring fastnesses, among which were those of the most powerful princes of the Dekkan. He was at length brought to a check by the garrison of Gōndikotta, to which he had been attracted by the reputed wealth of the great temple; the treasury whereof was said, in oriental language, to be deep enough to contain a thousand square *kōs* of territory. The gallant Nur Singh Raj commanded the place at that time; but after having undergone all the most rigorous extremities of a protracted siege, he was compelled to yield, and became tributary to Hydrabad.

There were some excellent specimens of Oriental tactics in the campaigns which followed. Venkutputti, king of Bijanuggur, had removed his seat of government to the frontier post of Penkonda, in violation of his treaty with Mohummed Kooli Kootab Shah, and also made many aggressive incursions upon the Hydrabad possessions. In retaliation of these offences, the Hydrabad chief, having reduced Gōndikotta, marched directly upon Penkonda, and laid siege to it. After the lapse of a few days, Venkutputti sent an embassy to Mohummed Kooli Kootab Shah, for the purpose of negociating terms of peace; and an armistice, during the treaty, was an immediate result. The Hindoos, taking advantage of this cessation of hostilities, and the temporary absence of the Mohummedan troops from their lines, actively employed themselves in laying in supplies. In three days, they had procured stores sufficient for a prolonged siege; and before the suspicions of their enemies were excited, they had gained a reinforcement of troops, under the celebrated Jugdue Rao, amounting to nearly twenty thousand men. When the king of Hydrabad was informed of these faithless proceedings, he became greatly exasperated, and immediately renewed the siege with increased vigour. His utmost efforts were now, however, quite unavailing, and, as the monsoon approached, he feared to be cut off from his capital by the inundations of the Krishna; he therefore raised the siege, planting strong garrisons in all the forts which he had reduced; and, leaving a large force, as an army of observation, under the command of Mortaza Kahn, he withdrew to Hydrabad.

By these arrangements the district of Gōndbere was left altogether without protection, and Venkutputti, taking immediate advantage of this oversight, became, in his turn, the aggressor. He sent the Raja of Udgherridroog to make a diversion upon the rear of the enemy's forces, by laying waste the country; and Afzul Kahn, the governor of Gōndbere, finding that he had not a sufficient force to oppose the advance of the Hindoos, sent off such cavalry as he could muster, to retaliate, by an inroad, upon the Udgherridroog *jaghir*. This manœuvre had the desired effect; the Hindoos withdrew to protect their own country, and, coming up with Afzul Kahn, they surrounded his little force. At this juncture, according to a preconcerted scheme, Aga Kahn, with a party of five hundred cavalry, came stealthily upon the rear of the Hindoo army, and making a sudden charge, before the enemy could discover the weakness of his numbers, he put them completely to the rout; then Afzul Kahn, joining in the pursuit, succeeded in capturing the camp equipage, and took many prisoners. Upon this memorable occasion, the Hindoos actually lost no less than three thousand men, a number double the entire force of the Mohummedans.

The monsoon having set in, Venkutputti found an opportunity of augmenting his forces; so that when the floods abated, he took the field with an army amounting to a hundred thousand men. Having heard that Mortaza Kahn had secretly penetrated into the western quarter of his dominions, as far as the celebrated city of Koorpa, and had sacked its sacred temples and destroyed the idols, Venkutputti marched with ten thousand cavalry, and gave him battle, but was defeated. Meanwhile Mohummed Kooli Kootab Shah, having heard of the overwhelming force collected by the Hindoo chief, sent off a reinforcement to Mortaza Kahn, consisting of five thousand cavalry, under the notorious Roostum Kahn, who had orders to assume the general command of the army. The strength of the Hindoo army was, however, so great, that it was found impossible for the Mohummedans to give them battle; and Mortaza Kahn advised that their operations should be confined to plundering, and the most irritating system of predatory warfare. The vain Roostum affected to despise the council of his junior, and ridiculed his caution; nevertheless, he refrained altogether from engaging in any more decided mode of attack, and his folly and indecision speedily terminated in the total defeat of his army, and his own exposure and disgrace.

At the full moon of Bhadrapada (September), which has been appointed a holiday for all oxen employed for draught or burden, the Hindoos, in these parts, have a custom of painting and decorating with clothes and jewels all the largest and most lively of those animals, and leading them in procession in honour of Krishna. After certain ceremonies have been performed, the horns of the cattle are gilt, tassels and bells are affixed to them, and garlands of flowers and gaudy-coloured cloths are hung about them. Each of the farmers takes his team to the bazaar, and a procession being formed, the motley multitude of kine are led forth from the city gate, headed by bands of music, and accompanied by a vast concourse of peasantry; the cattle-owners are enveloped in various ludicrous disguises, singing, shouting, and throwing themselves into all sorts of absurd attitudes and frantic gestures. After proceeding to a certain distance, the beasts are set at liberty, and permitted to stray where they will. Unaccustomed to their freedom, they usually frisk, and fling, and gallop about in all directions, with a wildness which gives them the appearance of being mad. It happened, that at this particular season, Roostum Kahn was on a reconnoitering detour, with a small party of attendants, at a little distance from the army; and, as it had been provided by his evil destiny, he beheld a procession of the kind above-described, advancing towards him. Being ignorant of its meaning, his fears suggested to him that the strange scene was nothing less than an exhibition of witchcraft, and forthwith he galloped off to the rear in dismay, and, by his alarmed aspect, communicated a panic to his troops. They began immediately to disperse in all directions, and became entangled in the marshes. The Hindoo soldiery, who were upon a height commanding a view of the whole scene, observing the confusion in the Mohummedan army, soon surrounded them, and made them an unresisting prey to their marksmen. The Mohummedan army was thus almost annihilated; and Roostum Kahn, who was a notorious boaster, being recalled to Hydrabad, was degraded from his rank, and sentenced to that most odious and disgraceful of punishments, of being attired in the costume of a woman, and paraded through the streets of the city, mounted backwards upon an ass. He was afterwards banished from the kingdom.

The whole history of Mohummed Kooli Kootab Shah is full of interest. He wonderfully increased the prosperity and extent of his dominions, and was perhaps the most munificent of the Kootab Shahi sovereigns. According to the account of Meer Aboo Talib, he expended in the erection of public works, in Hydrabad alone, a sum amounting to £2,800,000 of English money; and distributed to the poor, from his private purse, an annual sum of £24,000. He died in A. D. 1611.

The streets of Hydrabad are narrow and inconvenient, and abominably dirty and noisy. The houses, for the most part, though extremely picturesque, are but slightly built, and many of them are entirely of wood. The handsome gateway on the left side of the Char Minar, as seen in the annexed view, forms the entrance to the Nizam's palace, which, with its numerous courts and gardens, occupies a large extent of this quarter of the city. The whole place has been lately much improved, in accordance with the European notions, by the present Nizam, Nasur-ud-Dowla; but there is still abundant need of reformation, especially in cleanliness and ventilation. The country around Hydrabad has a wild and barren aspect, and is intersected by a range of irregular hills of a remarkably rugged and jumbled appearance, as though they had recently been cast together by some violent convulsion and upturning of the earth.

The Nizam's court, being that of the principal independent Mogul sovereign in India, has preserved more than any other the ancient Mohummedan forms and ceremonies; but many articles of European manufacture, both of convenience and luxury, are made use of by the nobles of the court. The Nizam himself possesses immense magazines, in which are stored up innumerable bales, crates, and chests, containing all the presents which he has, from time to time, received from European powers. Cases of costly cloths, glass, china, machinery, clocks, watches, jewellery, bijouterie, and curiosities of every description, which have been accumulating during the past half century, are piled up all around the walls, but are never exhibited or permitted to see the light.

The merchants of Hydrabad are reputed to be very wealthy, and are, for the most part, persons of good family, of education, and influence. They are almost exclusively Mohummedans; but a traveller who visited the city about twenty years since, has given, in his sketches of India, an entertaining account of an eccentric Englishman who had established himself in the city, and enjoyed a thriving business. He writes:—"I passed one morning, and took tiffin with a famous English merchant, who holds a singular sort of *durbar* every morning, at which you see shroffs and merchants, officers and nobles, coming to beg, borrow, lend, or transact business; all which is done according to the native customs. These Mr. P. observes, in everything connected with his establishment; even when alone, to the sitting on the floor to a dinner served in their fashion; reading the Arabian Nights with his Moorish wives; and (*de gustibus non est disputandum*,) listening with pleasure to the musical sounds of the native *tom-tom*.

"He is a man of uncommon talent and great information,—very popular among the natives, of course, and with the British also, for his liberality, ready and obliging politeness, and unbounded hospitality to all; to the poor also he is very charitable. The choice of an Eastern mode of life is, with him, not altogether unnatural. He was born of a native mother, a female of Delhi, of good descent. He was sent to England as a boy for education, returned early to this country, and long commanded a large body of horse in the Dekkan, under native chiefs."

This man appears not merely to have assumed the Moslem costume and manners, but to have imbibed, almost without exception, that generous spirit of universal friendship, and free and profuse hospitality, which is, in truth, part of the character of the wealthy Mohummedan merchant; forming a strong contrast with the niggard, penurious habits of the same class of persons among the Hindoos. The trade is chiefly in precious stones, particularly diamonds; and all the principal dealers in these costly articles, as well as the bankers, have depositories for their treasures within the fort of Golkonda, for the sake of security. Hence, a common error has arisen, which has made Golkonda celebrated throughout Europe for its diamond mines; and some geographical works even go so far as to describe these mines; while, in very truth, the place produces no sort of gem,—all such merchandise being brought in a rough state from Balaghat, and the plains below the Neilgherri mountains, in the vicinity of the river Penna. They are there found in the greatest abundance, in an alluvial soil; but it is supposed that they have been brought down from the hills by the torrents, and deposited therein,—the sandstone breccia of the clay formation being the matrix.

This famous fortress is of a date so remote, that native antiquaries, when inquired of concerning it, content themselves by asserting that it has existed from the beginning. Certain it is, that long before the Kootab Shahi dynasty, it was the capital of the Bhamani empire, and for hundreds of years prior to that period was the seat of government under the primeval Hindoo princes. Until the introduction of European modes of warfare in India, the fortress had been deemed impregnable. It is situate upon an isolated rocky hill, and is defended by a succession of intricate lines of fortification, rising one over the other, upon the northern and eastern faces; the other sides are inaccessible to troops. At the base of the hill, an enormous advanced work, enclosing a space seven miles in circumference, occupies all the practicable ground. This work consists of a high and strong wall, furnished at the angles with bastions and towers, and surrounded by a dry ditch of ample dimensions; it is, however, too extensive to be defended except by a large army. Its palaces and mosques are now fast falling to decay; but the massive and yet elegant mausoleums of its former kings and princes appear likely to transmit the fame of its bygone might to many a future generation.

There is one small solid structure about half way between Hydrabad and Golkonda, which, about A. D. 1540, was raised to the memory of one Moollana Mohummed, who immortalised himself by boldly interposing between the great emperor

HUMMAIONE AND HIS MOOLLA,

or chief-priest, who in the discharge of his duty had innocently offended him. The circumstance, as told by Abul Fazil, was as follows:—

"When the Mogul army of Hummaione invaded the Dekkan, it marched under the personal command of that illustrious monarch, and with uninterrupted success, until they besieged the fortress of Tchampanier, where they were checked by the impregnable nature of the place. After a very protracted siege, they had given up all hopes of a surrender, when king Hummaione, heading an escalade party in person, stormed and carried the fort during the night. In order worthily to celebrate this heroic action, a festival was held, and the principal officers of the court and of the army were invited to a sumptuous entertainment at the royal tents. It was, however, impossible that all, both high and low, should be accommodated under the imperial canvas; and therefore, of course, the inferiors were excluded. These insignificant persons, being incensed at the supposed affront, agreed to meet and enjoy themselves in the Gardens of the Hallool. They did so, and quaffed the cup of pleasure, and the bowl of delirium, seasoning them with the bitter condiments of discontent, and mixing so little of the milk of moderation, that amidst their sallies of rude mirth, and ribald wit, they speedily began to load their superiors, respecting not even the Sultan himself, with loud invectives, and coarse treasonable abuse. Inflated with the fumes of wine, and the still more intoxicating vapours of conceit, the leader of the party took occasion to introduce the subject of the Zuffur Nameh, the history of Taimour, and proceeded to recite that passage in the early stage of the conqueror's fortunes, in which he is described as taking from each of his warlike followers,—at that particular time only forty in number—a brace of arrows, and, having bound them all together in a bundle,* to have passed them alternately to every individual, with a desire that each should use his utmost efforts to break them. When each had accordingly made the attempt without success, Taimour took the sheaf of arrows asunder, and returned to each person his own, which upon trial were, of course, easily snapped in two. Whereupon the renowned hero desired them to remember that as long as they, like the bundle of arrows, remained united, and firmly and faithfully bound to each other, few as they were in number, nothing would ever be able to put them down, and success and victory would inseparably attend them in all their undertakings. And this was, indeed, exactly confirmed by the event; for by making this simple and striking lesson the rule of their conduct, they finally rendered themselves masters of the fairest part of the habitable globe.

* This is evidently one with Æsop's fable of The Old Man and his Bundle of Sticks.

"Little reflecting that, morally speaking, the band of heroes, of whom the example was recited, might have been considered, individually, equal to an host, acting under the direction of divine Providence, towards the attainment of a particular object—the punishment of human depravity—these misguided men, with their senses steeped in wine, did not hesitate to place themselves on a footing of equality with warriors so renowned; not without arrogating to themselves a decided advantage in point of numbers, since, upon counting those present, they found that they amounted to no less than four hundred persons, in the pride of health and manhood. That very moment they accordingly quitted the imperial encampment in a body, for the purpose, as they conceived, of carrying their besotted plan of universal conquest into immediate execution, without taking into consideration the perils to which, at every step, they must inevitably be exposed.

"The day following, when it was observed that none of them were in attendance at their posts, and no information could be obtained as to the cause of their absence, a suspicion arose that they were not employed upon any very loyal or justifiable design. A division of a thousand cavalry was, therefore, immediately dispatched to look after them; and not very long afterwards, the whole of these infatuated visionaries were brought, bound hand and foot, to the imperial head-quarters. When it was announced to Hummaione that these pitiful truants were at his mercy, it happened to be Saturday, when, according to custom, being robed in ireful crimson, and seated upon the terrible *guddi* of judgment, he was occupied in passing sentence upon those who had been convicted of offence against the law. The nature of their crime having been declared, all these miserable men were immediately condemned to suffer punishment; the judge exercising in their sentences a cruelty of which there are few instances in the history of his government. Some were ordered to be trampled to death by elephants, some to lose their heads, others their feet or hands, others their eyes and tongues, while some, more fortunate, were permitted to escape with the loss of a few less important members, such as half-a-dozen toes or fingers, or perchance a nose and ears. But while the monarch was thus engaged in directing his vengeance against those who had dared to disregard his authority, the hour of evening prayer arrived; and the officiating Moolla, who was not particularly distinguished for his powers of discrimination, in the course of the first *rukkhât*, (general genuflexion,) unfortunately selected for the service that portion of the Khoran, entitled the Chapter of Elephants; relating to that circumstance in the history of Arabia, in which the tyrant Abraha, from Yemen, having despatched an army, accompanied by an extraordinary elephant, for the purpose of destroying the temple of Mekka, Alla is described as having employed a flight of gigantic cranes to stone his army to death. When, therefore, the course of the devotions had been concluded, Hummaione, conceiving that the Moolla had insolently selected this chapter with the design of charging him, by implication, with injustice and cruelty, directly gave orders that the unhappy man should be thrown at the feet of his infuriate elephants. Certain it is, that the executioners, being no respecters of persons, would promptly have carried the harsh mandate into effect, had it not been for the intercession of Moollana Mohummed, who, by bravely and generously casting himself between the despot's wrath and the innocent offender, ultimately succeeded in convincing the emperor of the simple character and unintentional error of the poor Moolla. Having thus removed the cause of his resentment, he went still further, and read him a severe lecture upon the unpardonable injustice and iniquity of lightly or angrily passing judgment, even upon the most culpable offenders; and with so great effect did this honest man urge his censure, his arguments, and advice, that the repentant monarch is represented as having passed the whole of the subsequent night in the most poignant regret and mortification of spirit." No one surely will consider that the bold and conscientious Moollana Mohummed had too much honour paid to his memory, at a time when the fame of a skilful barber, or of a successful cook, was often held aloft, for the admiration of future generations, by the erection of an elegant mausoleum.

Pursuing the road which runs under the walls of Golkonda from Hydrabad, the traveller, advancing in a north-westerly direction, is beguiled by some of the finest scenery of the Dekkan, until, having traversed about seventy miles, each stage increasing in picturesque beauty, he finds himself upon the summit of a bold table-land, overlooking the magnificent and renowned city of Bidur, which lies spread out before him, distant about a *kōs*. The scene is truly grand. The city itself, with its countless sky-piercing minarets and solemn domes, enclosed within a girt of dark embattled walls, covers a slight eminence in the centre of the picture. On the right, shrouded by a thick grove of wide-branching mango trees, is a cluster of princely-looking tombs, those of the ancestors of the present Nizam of Hydrabad; and on the left is the venerable ruin of the Madressa or College. Beyond the city, upon the plain, about a mile distant from the western gate, are to be seen the lofty cupolas which crown the splendid mausoleums of the Bereed dynasties of the ancient kings of Bidur. And, to close the picture, a fine well-cultivated champaign country, adorned with gigantic forest-trees, in endless variety, and watered by a thousand meandering streams, extending on all sides into the extreme distance, and only intercepted in rear of the town by the towering ruins of the ancient palaces, bounds the horizon.

The spot whence this scene first bursts upon the view of the traveller, is memorable as that whereon, four hundred years ago, was perpetrated a deed of sacrilegious violence, to which, according to pious notions of

THE SANCTITY OF A MOSLEM PRIEST,

a truly devout follower of the Prophet cannot allude, without an awe-inspired thrill; albeit the Prophet is represented as having executed an ample vengeance upon the malefactor. The facts, as gathered from Ferishta, are these:—

During the battle of Tumbola, wherein the army of Ahmud Shah Wulli Bahmuni, king of Bidur, had been engaged from the dawn of day until night-fall, in uninterrupted conflict with the doubly-numerous forces of Ahmud Shah Guzeratti, king of Gazerat, the day was repeatedly saved to the king of Bidur by the favour of one Saiud Nazur-ud-Deen Kurbali, a most holy man; who, having the spirit of prophecy, continually foretold the designs and manœuvres of Ahmud Shah Guzeratti, and thus enabled his prince to counteract them. After the close of night, both parties retreated towards their capitals, and Ahmud Shah Wulli Bahmuni suitably rewarded Nazur-ud-Deen, by conferring upon him five thousand *tunkas* of silver for his own benefit, and thirty thousand to be distributed in alms among the poor, and among the holy men, at Kurbala *. Having obtained his dismissal from the court, Nazur-ud-Deen was upon his road homeward, on horseback, and arrived about noon-day at the spot in question.

It happened that here one Shere Moolluk, an officer of high rank in the army of Ahmud Shah Wulli Bahmuni, and several of his comrades, were seated under the shade of the grove, enjoying each other's ribald wit, in concert with the bubbling of their *hookkas*. These reprobates, being well acquainted with the saintly character of the traveller who was passing them, continued nevertheless their noisy revels, and Nazur-ud-Deen, disgusted at the loose style of their conversation, spat upon the ground as he rode by them. Shere Moolluk, offended at this insult, called aloud to the traveller to dismount immediately, and with lowly reverence atone for his insolence. Now, as the Saiud took no heed, but continued to ride leisurely forward, the irate soldier commanded his men to drag him to the ground.

* This was the birthplace of Saiud Nazur-ud-Deen Kurbali, as denoted by the affixture to his name, and is a place of very great sanctity in Mesopotamia. According to Colonel Briggs, it is the spot whereon Hoossein, the grandson of the Prophet Mohummed, was killed, and where he lies interred.

Incensed at this outrage, Saiud Nazur-ud-Deen Kurbali rode back directly to the capital, and complained to the king, who pacified him, at the moment, by promising that the offence should never be forgotten, reminding him, with a mild rebuke for his want of proper confidence, that Alla and the Prophet would not neglect, on a fit occasion, to avenge his cause. Some time afterwards, upon the breaking up of the army, when it was customary to distribute honorary robes to distinguished officers previously to their return home, the king's eyes fell upon Shere Moolluk, and he recollected, in an instant, the infamous insult which that person had formerly offered to his favourite Saiud. He immediately gave orders that a certain infuriate elephant, named Kussab (the Butcher), should be brought, and, reminding Shere Moolluk of his impious conduct to Nazur-ud-Deen, ordered that he should be cast under the feet of that terrible animal, which, in one minute, crushed him as a pig would crush an egg; and he lay upon the ground, as lifeless as if his bones had been converted into dagger-hilts, and his skin into scabbards.

The Madressa was built by the renowned chief Mahmood Gawan, of whose untimely fate mention is made in a former page, under the description of

Penkonda. The foundation was laid about A.D. 1460, and the building was designed to form part of a magnificent square, which, upon the opposite side, contained also the great mosque, and many other public buildings; the whole having been erected by the same chief, and called after him the Gawan-ki-Chouk, but afterwards named by Aurungzebe the Turkt-Mahal. In the time of Ferishta, who was born A.D. 1570, this splendid range of buildings remained as perfect as if it had only just been completed; and, wonderful to relate, all the edifices were then still applied to the purposes for which they were designed by their founder. This lively historian, in enlarging upon the munificence of Mahmood Gawan, affirms that that hero was not only possessed of very extensive general knowledge, but that, unassisted, by dint of great perseverance, he had made himself master of many abstruse branches of learning and science. In mathematics and engineering he is said to have had no equal in his day; and he also evinced great taste in his literary compositions, a few of which are still existing. The most perfect is the Rozub-ul-Insha; but other poems, and fragments of descriptive composition, are preserved in the works of Moolana Jami Abdool Raiman, and of Moolla Abdool Kurreim Sihndi.

The nicety and great strength with which these elegant buildings were constructed, would doubtless have enabled them to have remained complete until

Painted by Wm. Taylor from a sketch by Captn. Meadows Taylor. Engraved by H. Watkins.

Madressa Budur

London. Published Oct. 1, 18[illegible], for the Proprietor, by Charles Tilt, 86, Fleet Street.

the present day, had it not been for the ravages of the despoiler, and the chance of war; for, after the capture of the city by the emperor Aurungzebe, at the close of the seventeenth century, the whole of this superb quadrangle was appropriated to the purposes of the invader's troops; the imperial halls were converted into barracks, and the Madressa itself was used as a powder-magazine. Alas! that it should have been so! As an evil destiny would have it, some powder was ignited, by an exasperated soldier, who, for the purpose of avenging himself upon a comrade with whom he was quarrelling, cast the burning *gools* * from his *chillaum* into a powder-cell. In a moment the whole magazine exploded, destroying the greater part of the beautiful building, and spreading destruction on all sides. Other accounts state the manner of the occurrence very differently. The traveller Thevenot, for instance, relates a tale which makes the explosion take place before the city had surrendered to Aurungzebe. He tells us that, when invested by that invader, it was governed by a veteran officer, a noble of tried fidelity and great courage, who indignantly rejected all the efforts of the Delhi emperor to corrupt him, and successfully kept him at bay for many days. A practicable breach was, however, at length made in the wall, and the signal was already given for the assault, when suddenly—as some affirm, by the fall of a

* Fire-balls used in the *hookka* to keep the tobacco burning.

rocket, or, as others insist, by the orders of the commandant, who preferred death to subjection—the magazine within the Madressa blew up, at a moment when the roof was covered with the garrison, who had assembled upon it for the purpose of selling their lives as dearly as possible. It is almost needless to add that all persons thereon perished : among them were the governor and his three sons.

It is certainly extraordinary that any uncertainty should exist concerning so signal an event, and one which occurred at no very remote period ; at a time, indeed, concerning which historians have, for the most part, been tediously explicit. Of the fact, however, there is no question ; indeed, evident traces of the shock are to be observed even to this day, and all relations agree in mentioning that so fearful was the explosion, that the massive vaulted roof was carried high in the air, and fell in a shower of stones upon the city ; moreover, the minaret, near which was stowed the great bulk of the powder, was seen to reel to and fro, till, losing its equilibrium, it fell against the ruined base of a neighbouring wall, and the beautiful shaft was shivered in twain about forty feet from its foundation. The lower part still stands in an inclined position, as seen in the accompanying plate. The other minaret remains entire, and presents a goodly specimen of what these magnificent erections once were. It is upwards of a hundred and thirty feet in height, and elaborately decorated with tablets, inlaid so as to form various elegant figures, in which sentences of the Khoran are inscribed in large white characters, three feet in height, upon an enamelled ground of green and gold.

The noble founder of this magnificent college had collected, during his adventurous and successful life, one of the most extensive libraries mentioned in the history of Hindostan. He bequeathed it to the Madressa for the use of the students, together with a great number of his own manuscripts and drawings; but it does not appear that there is any remnant of them left. Whether they were carried off and dispersed before Aurungzebe's time, or destroyed in "Aurungzebe's explosion," remains for the investigation of such as may be anxious to ascertain. Mahmood Gawan appears to have delighted more in the possession of his books, his elephants, and horses, than in all the vast magnificence and wealth which his royal master had so profusely lavished upon him. The following anecdote, related by Ferishta, confirms this assumption, and beautifully exemplifies his simplicity of character, and the genuine greatness of his mind.

Having been three years absent from the capital, in command of an arduous and almost hopeless expedition against Goa, and other possessions of the Rai of Bijanuggur, Mahmood Gawan returned to Bidur, covered with glory and renown, having achieved the most wonderful victories, and having carried unvaried success through all his most perilous undertakings. Immediately upon his arrival, Mohummed Shah hastened to receive him with all possible distinction, and actually condescended to honour him with the royal presence in the palace for a whole week, conferring upon him the very highest titles of a subject, with a suit of his own robes*. The queen-mother also did her utmost to magnify him in the sight of all men, by assigning to him the ineffably illustrious appellation of Brother. His favourites were made the favourites at court, and his chief servants were raised to be the chief servants of the state. Khoosh Kuddum, the commander of his elephants, for instance, who had behaved with distinguished gallantry in all his various campaigns, was promoted to high rank, with the title of Kishwa Kahn ; and the forts of Goa, Poonda, Kundwal, and Kolapoor, with tracts of the surrounding country, were granted to him in addition to his other estates. When Mahmood Shah took his royal leave of the general, who had now become prime-minister also, that chief retired to his own apartment, and divesting himself of the imperial robes, threw himself upon the ground, and wept plenteously. He then dressed himself in the humble habit of a dervish, and calling to his presence all those within the city who were most distinguished for their learning and piety, he distributed among them the greater part of

* See p. 88.

his money, jewels, and other available property, reserving to himself only his elephants, his horses, and his library; saying,—"Praise be to the merciful Alla, who has this day rescued me from the most imminent danger, who has preserved me from the destroying power of temptation." One Moolla Shumsh-ud-Deen, a very wise and holy Saiud, inquired of him the meaning of his extraordinary language, and the motive which had induced him to throw away his great wealth. The magnanimous chief thus replied:—"When the king condescended to become the guest of one so utterly unworthy as myself; when the queen-mother humbled herself by raising me to the exalted dignity of Brother in the royal household, my evil passions began to prevail against the influence of reason; the struggle between inclination and judgment, between vice and virtue, was so great in my mind, that my countenance became disturbed even in the presence of his imperial majesty, who thereupon tenderly inquired the cause of my emotion. I was compelled to feign illness as an excuse for my behaviour; and the king, advising me to take some repose, immediately returned to the royal palace. Having determined to release myself from the thraldom of the black pride which had entered my heart, I forthwith cast away my wealth as a principal temptation to evil." The great man moreover added, that he looked upon all of which he was possessed as, in truth, the king's, lent to him for a season only; and he therefore disposed of them in such a manner as might best advantage the state. The horses, and elephants, and books, he retained for further service.

From this day forth, Mahmood Gawan always wore the plainest apparel; and, when at leisure from the affairs of the state, invariably retired to his mosque and madressa, and spent his time in acquiring and imparting knowledge, selecting for his companions persons eminent for their piety and virtue. Every Friday evening he perambulated in disguise through the various wards of the city, and distributed alms to the poor, saying, as he bestowed his own bounty:—"The king gives you this." These acts are not regarded as eccentric by good Mohummedans, but as forming the noblest example for every virtuously disposed person.

The walls of Bidur are about seven miles in circumference; an extent of boundary which appears to have been, for some reason, probably superstitious, the favourite circuit of Mohummedan fortified cities all over India. These walls are built of dark red granite, are handsomely embattled, and have solid round towers and bastions at every angle. The gates, too, appear to have been originally protected by out-works; and the ditch which surrounds the whole has been hewn out of the solid rock. Upon the eastern side, the walls run in undulations following the inequalities of the ground; and here the citadel, raised upon a high mount, has a fine command over the whole works. On all sides the city is filled with noble remains of antiquity, which cannot fail to interest the visitor, especially him who is conversant with the history of the Bahmani and Bereed kings.

There is little commerce carried on in Bidur, and the principal article of manufacture is the beautiful metallic pottery known in India as the Biḍuri, or vulgarly the Vidri, ware, which is in great demand for the bottoms and mouth-pieces of hookkas, for vases, beetel-dishes, and other elegant household utensils. The ware defies all imitation, although the manufacturers make no secret of their art; the great nicety required in the preparation of the material, and skill in the *modus operandi*, being apparently unattainable, except to those who have been bred to it. The process is most ingenious, and appears to be practised only by Hindoos. The composition is of a fine dark-brown colour, almost black, but quite metallic in appearance, and if tarnished it is easily restored. It was until lately supposed to be formed from a metallic stone or lithomarga, strongly resembling the Biduri ware in colour and texture, which is to be found on the table-land of Bidur. But Dr. Heyne, the naturalist, assures us that this notion is erroneous,—he having visited the place with a sanguine expectation of discovering a new mineral; and having been disappointed by resolving the material into a certain earth, fused with twenty-four parts of tin and one of copper. This scientific traveller has given a minute description of the process of moulding and casting the vessels; and he then explains the colour to be given by a remarkably ingenious and somewhat mystic operation. He says:—"It consists in taking equal parts of muriat of ammonia and saltpetre earth, *such as is found at the bottom of old mud walls in old and populous villages in India*, mixing them together with water, and rubbing the paste which is thus produced upon the vessel, which has been previously scraped with a knife." He adds,—"The change of colour is almost instantaneous, and, what is surprising to me, lasting."

The method of inlaying the patterns of scrolls and flowers with which these articles are always ornamented, is also described by Dr. Heyne, and affords a good specimen of native patience and dexterity in such matters. "As nothing looks handsome in the eyes of an Indian, but what is glittering with gold and silver, it may be imagined that their *hookka* and beetel-dishes, which are chiefly used on festive* occasions, are not left destitute of these ornaments; they are chiefly decorated with silver in the forms of festoons, fanciful flowers, and leaves. Sometimes I

* The Doctor of course alludes to daily and hourly festivities; for a native does not willingly pass an hour without his *hookka* and *beetel-dan*.

have seen a little gold interspersed. The way of inlaying them is very simple ; but *of course* is as tedious as can well be imagined, and could be only practised where time is of little value. The parts of the projected figure are first cut out in silver leaf, and are placed in a piece of broken earthenware before the artist, who cuts with a pointed instrument the same figure on the vessel, applies the silver leaf, piece after piece, and gently hammers it into its place. The greatest skill is required in tracing the figures on the vessel exactly to correspond with those of the silver-leaf, and in this I have never seen them mistaken. They do their work very expeditiously, and will make any figure upon copper with the greatest nicety, according to the pattern which is laid before them." The practitioners of this art affirm that their knowledge of the manufacture was known to their forefathers, upon the same spot, upwards of two thousand years since, where primitive Hindooism had continued undisturbed from the time of the world's creation.

The road leading through the western gate of the city, traverses a fine plain, bounded by broad belts and patches of noble old mango trees, interspersed with Moslem buildings of infinitely varied forms. At the distance of about half a mile from the walls is the burial-place of the Bereed dynasty of the kings of Bidur. There are three principal tombs and a great many smaller ones ; but unfortunately, as none of them bear any inscription, except passages from the Khoran in the Arabic character, it is now impossible to decide with any certainty whose remains are laid beneath any one of them in particular. The largest, however, is generally reputed to be that of Ameer Bereed, who reigned for a period of forty-five years, and was the most powerful of the dynasty.

The origin of these kings is thus related by Ferishta * :—"Kasim Bereed Toork was brought by Shahab-ud-Deen to Bidur, and sold as a Georgian slave to Sultan Mahmoud Shah Lushkurri Bahmani, by whom he was admitted among the Georgian attendants of that monarch. In his reign, he distinguished himself by his bravery against the Maharhattas residing between Peitan and Chakun, whom he was deputed to reduce. One action, in particular, took place, in which Kasim Bereed was victorious, and having slain Sabaji Maharhatta, the king gave that deceased chief's daughter in marriage to Kasim Bereed's son, Ameer Bereed, as a reward for the hero's services. Sabaji's territory was also conferred upon him; and upwards of four hundred Maharhattas, who were connected with the late chief, entered his service; many of whom he persuaded to embrace the faith. To this attached body of Maharhattas Kasim Bereed always evinced the utmost kindness; and the connexion formed by his son's marriage gave him a

* Briggs's translation.

Drawn by G. Howse from a sketch by Captⁿ Meadows Taylor. Engraved by J. Redaway

Tombs of the Bereed Kings, Bidur

London Published Oct. 1, 1839 by Charles Tilt, 86 Fleet St.

paramount influence upon his estate; so that, in the reign of Mohummed Shah Bahmani, he, like many others of the nobles, aspired to regal power. By the connivance of Adil Shah, Nizam Shah, and Imad Shah, he usurped the government of the forts of Ousa, Kandahar and Oodghir; and leaving to his king the town and fort of Bidur only, he assumed independence, and read prayer and coined money in his own name, about the year A. D. 1491-2."

Upon the death of Kasim Bereed, which occurred in A. D. 1504, Ameer Bereed ascended the throne. During his rule Mahmood Shah Bahmani died, and the Bahmani crown descended to Oolla Shah, who was driven from his capital by Ameer Bereed. Thus was the Bereed Shahi dynasty established in Bidur. The royal dignity did not, however, long remain in the family; the government being wrested from Ameer Bereed's grandson, by a conspiracy of all the other princes of the Dekkan. It cannot but excite our surprise, then, that so short-lived a kingdom, and one of comparatively small importance, should have left so many magnificent monuments of its kings and ministers; for, in truth, these tombs excel in grandeur and costliness all others in the Dekkan.

In the annexed plate, the large mausoleum upon the right hand is that ascribed to Ameer Bereed; who is said to have designed it himself, and, according to a common custom among Mohummedans, to have had it built during his life-time. It is most elaborately carved within and without, the patterns containing numerous inscriptions of verses from the Khoran; and these in the interior are of blue enamel. This noble tomb was originally surrounded by a wall having three magnificent gateways, one of which remains perfect, and is seen in the centre of the picture. The others are still standing; but are not in so excellent a state of preservation.

> Man builds with the hand of time,
> God with the finger of eternity.
>
> NAZAMI.

NEILGHERRIES.

THE Neilgherri mountains are within the province of Koimbatoor, in Southern India, a little below the country of Maisore. They extend east and west, and form a connecting link between the Eastern and Western Ghàts. Geographers would rank them in the second class of mountains, the altitude of their highest peak being something less than nine thousand feet.

Here, amid the raging heats of the tropics, scarcely twelve degrees north of the equator,

> The breezy Spring
> Stands loosely floating on the mountain top,
> And deals her sweets around.

Hither, from the scorched and panting soil of the plains, from the smiting breath of pestilent junguls, the traveller may be transported, almost as speedily as the reader, to regions of perpetual vernal freshness and health. And here the wandering European meets a thousand fairy friends in the "langsyne" flowers which crowd upon his path. The violet, the primrose, the buttercup, and wild anemone, with countless varieties of the orchis tribe, throng every bank; the wild thyme, and the tall feathering fern, clothe the steep mountain side; while here the dog-rose, there the flowering woodbine, come peering through the clustered shrubs, to seek the genial sunshine. The woods are carpeted with familiar mosses and lichens, in endless variety of tints, down to the very edge of the prattling streamlet, which, dashing through the downward glen, gathers a thousand springs in its devious chase, until it plunges, a gushing torrent of foam, over some hanging precipice. Now, intercepted in its giddy flight by a projecting rock, the broad volume is scattered into many broken channels, and creeps away through the sheltering underwoods; now, in numberless cataracts, it once more leaps a jutting cliff, and mingles all its waters in a foaming pool. How unlike INDIA! In all of these, in every light, in every shadow, a host of airy tongues whisper the names of places and of people which all dissolve into that one word, Home. Yet soon the vision fades, as the eye follows the course of the swelling stream. Away it glides in a soft murmuring current, more broad, more smooth, more slow, through darkening shores, through sultry forests, and the desert wild, down to the basking plains. But a hasty glance, a hasty thought, of perils past and miseries escaped, refills the measure of delight, and the imagination weaves once more the happier picture of "sweet home," from "the large aggregate of little things" which crowd upon the memory, and speak of bygone times.

Whence came these pleasant scenes? is the natural question of the admiring traveller; and if a well-informed Koimbatoori be within earshot, he will be answered—"From the moon." Yes, verily, from the moon! says the legend current among the Hindoos of Koimbatoor; for the god Ram, being in pursuit of his enemy Ravana, who, it is well known, had forcibly carried off the divine goddess Sita, sped through the vaulted heavens, having his sword drawn, ready to deal the death-blow of revenge. In the forgetfulness of his direful wrath, lo! by an incautious wave of his mighty weapon, he struck the moon with the point thereof, and severed from the face of that beauteous globe a chain of verdant mountains, which immediately fell to the earth, in the province of Koimbatoor, and united the Eastern and Western Ghâts. Hence came the Chandaghirri [Mountains of the Moon], a name which was subsequently changed by the auspicious Ram to Neilgherri [Blue Mountains], because he could not endure to be reminded of his awkward mischance. If the hearer be incredulous, the ingenious Koimbatoori will speedily apply an argument for the subversion of his scepticism, which he believes to be incontrovertible:—Let him look upon the moon when three or four days old, and he will see, upon her unequal disk, the very spot from which the Neilgherries were cut off. The horns are seen to project beyond the unillumined portion of the sphere, exhibiting what the English peasant calls "the old moon in the new moon's arms," and this imperfect part of the circumference is that whence came the Neilgherries. If the philosopher endeavour to explain the optical illusion, the Koimbatoori listens politely to the end of his exposition, and then tells him that his argument must go for nothing, since he himself must have been convinced, even though unconverted, by the more simple and comprehensible tale of Ram and Ravana.

The Neilgherries are inhabited by three distinct races, who call themselves aborigines; the Kotas, the Burgas, and the Thodas. These several tribes hold themselves entirely apart, the one from the other, except as the Burgas are tenants of the Thodas, in whom is the right of soil. They appear to emulate dissimilitude in all things, although apparently free from jealousy or aversion. Their abodes, their laws, their language, their religion (if a faint notion of a supreme Power may be so called), their habits and pursuits, their costume, their very persons, are almost as dissimilar as it would be possible to make them. The Kotas, forming about a tenth part of the whole population, are a wretched, insignificant, degraded race; unsightly in person, whose intellect can scarcely be said to amount to anything more than instinct, and who are governed by few laws except those of the brute creation.

The Burgas are the most numerous class, are somewhat more personable, and apparently more cleanly, though it is questionable if they be much more civilised than the Kotas. They are the cultivators of the soil, and are a very industrious race, notwithstanding they are said to have sprung originally from the inert Hindoos. In person they are diminutive, but active; the countenance is far from intelligent, though mild, and the complexion is fair. Both sexes would be vastly more engaging if they could be taught the luxury of cleanliness; but, alas! like the *paharris* of the Himálas, they are said to wash but once in seven years. The costume of the women, though very original, also appears susceptible of improvement, inasmuch as discomfort and unsightliness would seem to have been the desiderata of the invention. It consists of a peculiar style of petticoat—to call it rude, to call it uncouth, barbarous, would give no adequate notion of its incongruous discomfort and unsightliness—made of the very crudest description of coarse hempen-cloth, in the fashion of an elongated sack, but open at bottom. Being tied by a running string immediately under the arms, it descends to the ancles, leaving the neck, shoulders, and arms, bare; and again it is confined at the knees, in the same manner, by a second string;

so that it is impossible for the wearer to take an extended step, the extreme inconvenience of which, in a mountainous country, may be readily conceived.

The villages of the Burgas are as singular, and apparently as comfortable, as the apparel of the females. They are built upon the hill-side, so as to form three faces of a square, with the open side towards the valley; the whole range being divided into cots, the dimensions whereof must certainly require that the inmates, considering their usual numbers, should be stowed away in layers reaching to the roof. What the arrangement may really be I am unable to declare, but certain it is, that in the evening when all have returned home, however full the huts may seem to be of chattering men, the common square is filled with scolding women and naked screaming children. Yet at night all have retired within their narrow domiciles, and nothing would indicate the presence of so great a multitude, save a loud yet stifled noise, which might be taken for the hard breathing of the gigantic Ram, suffering under the oppression of an elephantine night-mare.

The Thodas are in every respect superior to their fellow-mountaineers, the Kotas and Burgas, partaking more of the character of highlanders, being equal in stature to Europeans, nearly as muscular, enjoying hardy constitutions, excellent intelligence, and having withal regular, handsome, Roman features, with fine clear brown complexions, and full beards. Their deportment is remarkably frank and easy, their dispositions generous, and their manners altogether peculiarly agreeable to Europeans, because free from the fulsome sycophancy of the Hindoos. Their costume somewhat resembles the Roman toga, and consists of one piece of cotton cloth wound round the body, leaving the right arm at liberty, and thrown over the left shoulder. Indeed, altogether there is a striking resemblance to the ancient Romans about these singular people; quite sufficient, certainly, to encourage the research of the curious. True it is that they believe themselves to be aboriginal inhabitants of these mountains; but they have no history of their forefathers, no sort of records, no remnants even of tradition, and scarcely any religion, except a few vague notions which have evidently been borrowed from the Hindoos. They possess no knowledge of writing, and their language is said to have no affinity, either in root or inflection, to any other Oriental tongue. When, to all these circumstances, we add that, in several parts of Southern India, Roman* and Byzantine coins, and other relics, have been discovered, I cannot but think that their Roman origin may be fairly suspected; at all events, the speculation must be well worthy of scientific investigation.

* In A. D. 1800, a Roman urn was discovered below the foundation of an ancient building at Palasi, in Koimbatoor, containing a great many coins of Augustus and Tiberius, which are, I believe, now in the possession of the East India Company. This is one instance only among many such discoveries.

These Thodas are a pastoral people, subsisting entirely upon the produce of their buffaloes, which they keep in immense herds, migrating from place to place for the sake of pasture. Their villages are usually built in an open glade, sheltered above on two sides by a hanging wood, and the spots appear always to be selected with an eye to the beauties of the scenery. The huts are curious,—being built of small boughs of trees, interlaced in a form like the tilt of an English waggon, and then thatched; the walls being woven with twigs, and plastered with mud. For the sake of warmth, the doors to these cabins are made so small, that it is difficult to imagine how the sturdy highlanders, even on their hands and knees, can creep into them. One large hut of this kind in the centre of the village serves the double purpose of a general dairy and a temple of worship. The Thoda women are comely in countenance, and of a graceful figure. During the season of emigration, they visit Ootakamund and other European settlements, and perambulate the place with mountain fruits for sale. They are most amusingly inquisitive, and require little encouragement for the gratification of their curiosity. Among them, as indeed is the case in all the mountainous countries of India, polygamy prevails, without any appearance of jealousy or disunion. Whether this singular fact be referable to any disparity in the numbers of the respective sexes among the mountaineers of India I am unable to say; but surely it

Painted by T. Creswick from a sketch by Capt. Meadows Taylor | Engraved by J. W. Archer

Kooner Pass, Neilgherri Mountains

cannot be attributable, as other travellers have suggested, to peculiarity of climate or physical constitution? This, too, I leave for the decision of the more learned.

The spot from which the annexed view has been taken is in the Koonoor pass, near the second milestone, having Hulli-kul-Droog upon the right, and, in the distance, the plains of Koimbatoor, through which the diminishing stream of the second Bhowani winds like a silver thread. The rugged steeps of Hulli-kul-Droog,—here assuming every diversity of fantastic configuration of which wood and rock are susceptible, there spreading soft undulating pastures to the sunshine,—sweep down to the boiling torrent and thundering cataracts of Koonoor. Upon its lofty summit is a little fort, enjoying a grand command over all the surrounding country. This was built by Hyder Ali, and was used by him, and subsequently by his son Tippoo, as a place of confinement for state-prisoners. As a military work it is unimportant; for, though almost inaccessible to troops, it defends nothing, nor could a garrison stationed therein be available for any service, except the defence of the fort itself. It has long since been abandoned to the birds and beasts of the forest, and it could hardly be better appropriated.

The soil of the Neilgherries is naturally productive, and is susceptible of the highest cultivation; especially in the lowlands, where the Burgas raise luxuriant crops, without more labour than is necessary just to scratch up the surface, so as to cover the seed; neither tilling nor dressing is bestowed upon the land, yet the harvest is plentiful; and neither frost, nor snow, nor deluge, nor drought, are known to come unseasonably, to interfere with the regular operations of the husbandman. Wheat, barley, oats, small pulse, and potatoes, have been grown with abundant success in the neighbourhood of Ootakamund, an invalid dépôt, which was established a few years since by the British government; and despite the earnest assurances of the Burgas, that the sacred mountains would return no produce to any but the devout worshippers of the divine Ram, it has been discovered that the presiding genius is, in truth, unusually bountiful in repaying the toil of European cultivators.

MERAT.

> We the globe can compass soon,
> Swifter than the wandering moon.
>
> MIDSUMMER NIGHT'S DREAM.

THE little city of Merat was, in days long past, prior to the Mohummedan invasion, greatly renowned for the bravery and warlike disposition of its inhabitants. In A. D. 1019, it offered an heroic though ineffectual resistance to the invader Mahmood of Ghizni, who was then upon his march against Kunäoge; and it would appear that the gallant little garrison had something worth defending; for, beside an immense treasure in gold, silver, and jewels, they are said to have possessed, in their zenanas, a host of the most lovely women of Georgia and Circassia. According to the history of the times, it is only wonderful that the place could show any sort of opposition to Mahmood; for he is represented as commanding an army as countless as the atoms of air, whose movements were swift as lightning, and before whom the most magnanimous troops were dispersed like the frailest-winged insects before a hurricane. This conqueror was undoubtedly endowed with many of the most splendid and exalted qualities which can adorn and dignify the character of man; for his courage, his clemency, his religious ardour, (if, without profanity, Moslem bigotry may be so quoted,) and his charity, are extolled as without precedent. Eastern historians also reckon, among his glorious attributes, his insatiable desire of conquest and love of power, as it gave him, say they, extended means of improving the condition of the human race. Certain it is, that he was the warmest patron and lover of the arts, Akbur, perhaps, excepted, who ever attained to any great sway in Hindostan. Though economical in all other things, his bounty appears to have been bestowed without measure for the encouragement of civilization and refinement. The inscription which was placed over the remains of this monarch contained an ingenious play upon the letters recording the date of his death, similar in construction to that of Mohummed Shah Bhamani, before mentioned. The lines ran thus:—

شهي والاقدر سلطان محمود
چوشدازامر حف رحلت كزيني
بپرسيدم زها تف سال تاريخ
ندا امد كه شد جنت نشيني

bearing a literal translation thus:—*When the illustrious Sultan Mahmood, according to the will of God, went on his long journey, I inquired of a courtier the date of his decease, and a voice answered—" His place is in heaven*." The letters forming the last two words, جنت نشيني, if read as numerals, will give the date of his death—*Zikad*, 19, A.H. 873.

In the early part of the thirteenth century, Merat was invested by the army of Turma Kurreem Kahn, a descendant of, and the seventeenth prince in succession to, the illustrious Genghis Kahn; but the good fortune and courage of the garrison, this time, prevailed, and the besiegers were driven off, after suffering immense losses. Their wonderful success on this occasion, however, appears to have taught them an arrogance of conduct, which was the ultimate cause of their ruin, and of the total destruction of their ancient stronghold; for, in the year 1399, when that ruthless conqueror, Taimour, had rendered his name terrible throughout India, by carrying the worst horrors of pillage and bloodshed into the proud city of Delhi, the very heart and lifespring of Hindostan, the people of Merat laughed to scorn that warrior's ambassadors, and returned them with a message to the effect that they who had repulsed the attacks of so great a person as Turma Kurreem Kahn, would not condescend to notice the presence of so obscure a pretender as Taimour.

Taimour immediately despatched several of his most powerful Omras, among whom was the celebrated Roostum Toghai Boorga, with a large force, to invest the city; but these chiefs, on their arrival before the place, found that the garrison had prepared for a determined resistance, and had acquired the co-operation of three very formidable neighbouring powers. With these was a *gaubur* or infidel Rajhpoot, named Zuffi, whose numerous followers, rendered invulnerable by a process of sorcery, and skilful beyond example as marksmen, now lined the walls. Information to this effect was immediately carried to Taimour, who, enraged by their previous insolence, and this unexpected increase of strength, immediately placed himself at the head of ten thousand chosen horse, and, marching during the whole of the night, appeared before the gates of the city at noon on the following day. On the very moment of his arrival, the indefatigable Taimour gave orders that every commander, from his particular position, should immediately open a trench of approach towards the opposite point of the enemy's walls; and by these means, ere nightfall, a lodgment had been effected parallel to, or at the foot of, every tower or salient angle of the city. Terrified at the alarming celerity with which, in defiance of their most strenuous efforts, the besiegers succeeded in carrying on their approaches, the garrison appeared suddenly to lose all power of resistance; and of this their assailants did not fail to take immediate advantage. One of the chiefs, Alla-ud-Dad, followed by his brave band, advanced beneath the principal gate; and an intrepid fellow, named Serai, having tied his *kummurbund* *, or waist-band, in a noose, by a skilful cast affixed it to one of the battlements of the parapet, and immediately ascended to the top of the wall. Here he encountered Elaias, the Afghan, who being a famous swordsman, had like to have slain him; but he was quickly supported by his comrades who followed; and, as the numbers increased on both sides, a desperate struggle ensued, in which the *gaubur* chief was slain. A panic immediately spread through his hitherto dauntless followers, which being communicated to the rest of the garrison, the gates were thrown open to the besiegers, almost without opposition, and every man was speedily put to the sword. Thus, in a few short hours, a fortress which had defied the puissance of Turma Kurreem Kahn, fell before the spirit of Taimour and his veteran legions.

As a mark of his vengeance, Taimour gave the city up to the plunder of his troops, and then, with his own hand, planted a torch in the most combustible place, on the windward side. The conflagration spread even to the last house, consuming all but the citadel and fortifications. These were partially overthrown by the soldiers, at the command of their chief; but some were found so solid as to defy their utmost efforts, and are standing at this moment. Beyond these shapeless remains, patched and re-

* Usually composed of about twenty yards of muslin, which can be rolled up like a rope.

fitted when the town was subsequently rebuilt, there is nothing within the walls to interest the traveller; but in the neighbourhood, there are several Mohummedan tombs and ruined mosques, which attract notice. One of these, the most worthy, is here exhibited to the reader. It is called by the people of the place, Aboo's Moohkburra, or the resting-place (the common name for a tomb) of Aboo. But who this particular Aboo really was, all the various deponents whom I examined, could not say. During my eager inquiries upon this subject, no less than forty-five or forty-six illustrious Aboos were enumerated; concerning each of whom some piece of history, some tale, or romance, is recorded. Yet, strange to say, it did not appear probable to me, that any one of all the numerous Aboosso mentioned, should have been buried at Merat, when this mausoleum was erected.

If the date were not so very far back, the strongest suspicion would naturally attach to one Aboo Bukkur, entitled by some historians the key-stone of the power of Al Razi, who lived in A. D. 938; for of him it is written, that he was thrice buried. Indeed he appears to have lived a sort of triune existence, which should have entitled him to three such tombs. He was three times vizier, under three different khalifs; he performed three pilgrimages to Mekka; thrice fairly copied the sacred text of the Khoran; and, as before mentioned, was three times interred.

Drawn by C. Gibbon from a Sketch by T. Bacon Esq.

Engraved by ... Finden

Aboo's Tomb, Meratt.

London. Published Octr. 1. 1839. by Charles Tilt. 86. Fleet Street.

A still more interesting Aboo was Aboo Obaida, one of three eminent men of the same name, son of the glorious Mussaoa, and father of the never-to-be-forgotten Mohktaur. In A.D. 1634, this extraordinary Aboo was entrusted with the command of an expedition to invade Persia, and proved himself one of the bravest, though not the most discreet, of all the Aboos that have ever lived. After distinguishing himself by some of the most glorious feats of arms which emblazon the pages of Moslem history, Aboo Obaida succeeded in establishing himself on the banks of the Euphrates, and pitched his camp immediately opposite to that of the Persian army, leaving only the breadth of the river between the two great hostile multitudes. Now the Persian forces amounted, according to the most credible authorities, to eighty thousand, while those of Aboo were but nine thousand; but notwithstanding this, to others, appalling numerical disparity, Aboo forced the passage of the river, and gave battle to his enemy. Each hero who composed an unit in the incomparable troops of Aboo was at all times prepared and eager to engage ten hostile men; but they all confessed themselves quite unaccustomed to encounter hostile elephants; and when the advance of the Persian line was seen covered by an innumerable array of those warlike animals, something like confusion and dismay was to be detected in the conduct of Aboo's followers. Ever fearless, however, that godlike chief smiled upon the coming foe; and, with a word of allusion to the undying deeds of past days, he rallied the wavering valour of his men.

Near the centre of the Persian line, upon a monstrous white elephant, conspicuous among the multitude, no less from its size than from its colour, sat the commander of the forces, the illustrious Sheheriau, in a splendid *hàoda;* him did Aboo select as his antagonist, and, closely followed by his troops, advanced to the engagement. Having escaped untouched from a thick discharge of javelins aimed at his eminent person, Aboo made his assault; and, receiving the weapon of his opponent upon his shield, by a dexterous blow of his battle-axe, he cut asunder the ropes which bound the *hàoda* upon the elephant's back, and brought Sheheriau to the ground. By a second blow, dealt with the velocity of lightning, with the accuracy of fate, and with the force of an earthquake, Aboo clove the commander of the Persians asunder, from the crown of his head to his hips. The infuriate elephant, seeing his lord thus slaughtered before his face, directed all his terrible powers against the daring assailant; but Aboo, by a nice sweep of his axe, struck off the brute's proboscis. Yet, alas! in that act, his foot slipped in the gore of the prostrate Sheheriau, and he fell to the ground. Before he could recover himself, the gigantic animal, mortally wounded, was also falling; now casting his huge body forward, in a wilful spirit of vengeance, he crushed the immortal Aboo Obaida, as a fly is crushed under a barrel of honey.

There was likewise the incomprehensible Aboo Nudjedar, of A.D. 657; whose daring exploits are too miraculous to be calmly perused by the sensible reader. There were three equally distinguished Aboo Saiuds, and seven no less astonishing Aboo Alis, besides Aboo Jafiers, Aboo Mirzas, Aboo Abdallas, Aboo Shujas, and other Aboos in duplicate and triplicate, all of extraordinary merit. But, after all, perchance, the best method of giving the reader a faint impression (no more can be hoped) of the glory of the Aboos, will be to relate the circumstance which attaches an interest even to the lowliest and least meritorious of all the Aboos; and then to leave the identity of the particular Aboo of Merat, looming the more important in the dim perspective of mysterious uncertainty.

Aboo Akkur was a slave in the royal household of the ever-memorable Ameer Ishmael, and his name has been preserved through the following incident. Ishmael having defeated the army of Omar Lais,* captured that chief owing to the fiery spirit of his charger, which bore him headlong into the enemy's ranks; but the conqueror was still unable to possess himself of the great treasure which he knew was somewhere concealed in the capital; and he therefore inquired personally of Omar where it might

* Brother of the celebrated Yakoob Lais. See page 142.

be found. The captive replied, that before the engagement he had sent all the wealth of himself and his followers to Herat, lest it should fall into the hands of his enemies. Ishmael considered that the property had become his by right of conquest; and immediately marched to Herat, and demanded that it should be delivered up; but receiving no satisfactory reply, he laid siege to the city, and the inhabitants surrendered on express conditions of immunity. Still the treasure was not to be found, and his followers, being in arrears, became clamorous for pay; so that their commander was again compelled to put them off with promises. At last, the necessities both of the officers and men becoming exceedingly urgent, it was intimated to their chief, that the population being very large, he might raise an ample sum by levying a trifling tax upon each man. The virtuous Ishmael, with a rectitude which reflects unfading lustre upon his memory, rejected with scorn the dishonourable proposal, observing that, having pledged himself to protect the people, nothing should induce him to exact from them the smallest article of their property. Then, lest his followers should infringe, without his licence, the terms of treaty which he had made with the Heratis, he withdrew his camp to a distance from the place. Here his generals again assailed him with importunities on the same subject; when he addressed them in these memorable words:—"That great Being, who, with the lash of destiny, impelled the horse of Omar Lais to place his rider at my disposal, is also able to supply the wants and repair the decayed equipments of my soldiers, without the guilt on my part of a breach of faith with his creatures." This right confidence and honourable forbearance soon obtained its reward.

One of the ladies of Ishmael's family had taken off her necklace of rubies, and laid it upon the ground, while her attention was engaged by her infant. A kite, which happened to be hovering near, pounced upon and carried off the necklace, probably believing it to be a piece of meat. Aboo Akkur, who fortunately observed the robbery, immediately took horse, and watched the motions of the plunderer. After a long flight, the kite, finding himself disappointed in the value of his prize, let it drop from his talons, and it fell, as the finger of Providence directed, into a neighbouring well, in which there was at that time no water. Aboo Akkur forthwith dismounted, and caused himself to be lowered into the well, by means of the leathern bucket and windlass which was attached to it, and he soon discovered the necklace; but not the necklace alone, for, at the bottom of the well, he found a vast cavern, in which were deposited a great number of chests and bales of goods, piled together. On examining these, he found them to be filled with gold, and silver, and costly jewels, to an incalculable amount. So, remounting his horse, he returned to the camp of his master, and informed him of his wonderful discovery. The treasures were proved to be those of Omar Lais, which his kinsman of Herat had conveyed thither, as to a place of security ; and thus Ishmael was enabled to satisfy the necessities of his followers, while he inculcated, with better effect than before, his moral lesson. Aboo Akkur was made, from that day, a wealthy man, and was no less remarkable for his open-handed charity than for his good-fortune.

Merat was, for a length of time, the residence of two Brahminical impostors, who, not long since, became notable throughout Hindostan for the ingenuity and audacity with which they carried on their iniquitous system of plunder. The names of these pillaging priests,

SHRI GOOROO AND GOPA SHAHIR,

passed into a by-word, which remains to this day, denoting any fraudulent combination. One of the most daring and successful of their impositions was plotted against a wealthy Raja, celebrated, far and wide in India, for his religious enthusiasm, and the unbounded liberality with which he entertained all those Brahminical devotees and pilgrims who claimed* his charity. In relating the story, it will

* They never beseech, but demand, alms in the name of Brahma.

be necessary to premise, that the romance of Hindoo chronology divides the history of the world into four eras. The first is the *Satia Youg*, or age of purity and truth, during which the life of man was extended to a period of a hundred thousand years. The second is called the *Trita Youg*, that is, the age wherein one-third part only of mankind had become reprobate, and the term of man's life was then ten thousand years. The third is the *Dwapur Youg*, in which one-half of the human race became depraved, and the length of life one thousand years. And the fourth is the present age, the *Kali Youg* (literally evil age), in which mankind have become altogether vicious and impure, as well as short-lived. The fraud was thus effected :—Prior to the commencement of active operations, during a period of two or three years, Shri Gooroo and Gopa Shahir suffered their hair, and beards, and their finger-nails, to grow to a prodigious length, in order that they might the better represent the extraordinary characters they were about to assume. Shri Gooroo undertook to act the part of an ancient ascetic of the *Trita Youg*, and upon Gopa Shahir devolved the character of the disciple of this wonderful relic of remote ages.

They excavated a small tumulus in a remote and unfrequented quarter of the Raja's dominions, wherein Shri Gooroo was to suffer a living burial ; and having planted wild shrubs and jungul underwood around the entrance of the cave thus formed, they left their work for a season, until the plantation had acquired the appearance of an untrodden wilderness. All preliminary matters being arranged, Gopa Shahir bedaubed himself with oil and ashes, and went to the palace of the Raja, demanding an audience. Being admitted to the presence, he commenced a mournful complaint, crying out,—"O Raja, my heart is breaking with bitter affliction. The venerable preceptor and guide of my childhood is, I fear, for ever lost to me;—give me immediately a host of your followers to seek for him."

"Reverend father," replied the Raja, "who art thou? Who is thy preceptor? How was he lost to you? How can he be recovered? Speak, and depend upon my assistance."

"O Raja, in the *Trita Youg* I and my revered instructor lived together in a subterranean cell; and, hearing of the great god Ram's projected voyage to Lanka (Ceylon) in search of his goddess Sita, we commenced the performance of very fearful austerities in aid of his adventure. Unwilling to afflict my beloved guide by my presence during the infliction of these severities, I retired to a neighbouring cavern, and in the anguish of what followed I fainted; nor did I recover from the deadly swoon until a year or two since, when, alas! I found myself in the course of the *Kali Youg*. Shortly after my resuscitation, the god Ram appeared to me in a vision, and informed me that the venerable sage, whom I reverenced almost as a divinity, was also in the land of the living,—having survived, like myself, in a trance caused by the severity of his religious exercises, and the profundity of his meditations; but that he had not yet been recalled to the presence of life. What I demand of you, O Raja, is a large party of your subjects to search for his retreat, which I am aware is within the limit of your dominions. I am dying with anxiety once more to embrace him, and to give to this darkened age a light of intelligence and sanctity, which will obscure the sun at noon-day, and shed divine peace and happiness into the hearts of all degenerate mortals of the present race."

The righteous Raja was greatly agitated with the excess of his religious zeal, on hearing this extraordinary relation; and, turning to his assembled chiefs, he said,—"Truly I am greatly astounded at this wonderful disclosure; but how fortunate, or rather how miraculously favoured, am I, that so holy a being should have rested in my territories; and that I or my subjects should endeavour to render him a service! Let us forthwith commence our search."

Hereupon the Raja set out with a large body of labourers; and, attended by all his retinue of state, determined to continue the pursuit until the holy devotee was brought back to life; doubtless anticipating no end of spiritual promotion and advantage, in return for the good office he hoped to fulfil, as the deliverer of one so wonderfully influential with the divine Ram as this *fakhir*. Having collected his followers, he commenced in the neighbourhood of his capital, upturning every mound and hillock to be met with, and eagerly following in person the operations of the workmen; lest, by absence, he should be irrevocably deprived of the first glance of the recluse,—a glance which might be supposed to extend backward, into thousands of years antecedent.

Gopa Shahir, who directed the operations of the men, kept them three months employed at a distance from Shri Gooroo's retreat, encouraging the hopes of the credulous Raja, from time to time, by the relation of pretended visions and revelations; until, as he gradually approached the true position of his accomplice, he wound the whole multitude up to an extraordinary frenzy of superstitious expectation. At last, after cutting through several feet of solid earth, they opened a small cavern, from which came a rush of fresh air; and wherein, after an aperture had been made sufficient to admit the daylight, they discovered the ancient ascetic, cross-legged, immoveable, and with his eyes fixed as if in a profound trance. Gopa Shahir was the first to enter the cave, and by applying a small vial of consecrated extracts to the nose and eyes of his spiritual guardian, he restored him to consciousness. Gopa Shahir now exhibited every imaginable demonstration of ecstatic but reverential delight.

"O most holy servant of the great Ram," said he, "behold the Raja of these dominions has approached to pay his reverence. Be pleased to extend to him some token of your favour, in return for the devotion with which he has sought your presence."

"Has the divine Ram recovered the Goddess Sita?" inquired the holy man, without deigning to notice the speech of his pupil.

"Yes," replied Gopa Shahir, "he recovered the goddess, after a desperate struggle with Ravana. But these things, most holy father, are of ancient date; for, you have yet to learn that during the period of your meditations, the *Trita Youg* and the *Dwapur Youg* have both passed away; and, alas! I have to disclose to you that it will now be our misfortune to terminate our pilgrimage in the fallen age of *Kali*."

"Oh! horrible, horrible!" cried Shri Gooroo, covering his face with his hands, and exhibiting every indication of intense dismay. "Impossible! I shall never be able to exist in this degenerate age—the *Kali Youg!* was it not a by-word of infamy! who can survive this fearful misfortune? Alas! alas! I can only renounce all contact with the world, and retire to Kasi,* where the influence of depravity can never be felt."

On hearing these words, the devout Raja became exceedingly distressed, and entreated that the holy

* The ancient name of Benares.

man would condescend to consecrate his dominions, at least, by a temporary residence in his capital; but Shri Gooroo remained inexorable, and declared that nothing would tempt him to exist in such a world of sin and misery. He then inquired, with great anxiety, if the Goddess Gunga (the Ganges) still dwelt upon earth; and, being assured that she did, he demanded to be shown some of the water of the sacred stream. When it was brought to him, he beheld it with the most ineffable contempt, and cried, "O thou false and deceitful Raja! callest thou this water from holy Gunga? Yet, why should it not be, after all; for undoubtedly all things are now deteriorated. Behold, said he, what the goddess was, in the days of the *Trita Youg*." Hereupon, he showed them some of the milk which remained in his bowl.

The veneration of the Raja was greatly increased, on hearing the wonderful words of the *fakhir;* and, falling at his feet, he cried, "O most illustrious of mortals, how miserable am I, that I should be thus deprived of the holy counsels and society of so sacred a being, the contemporary of the divine Ram, and of the blessed sages, at the very moment when I had thought my good fortune to be in the ascendant! If however, you must, indeed, depart, condescend to receive from me some token of my devotion; of this small merit you must not deprive me. Gopa Shahir here joined in the intreaties of the Raja; reminding

Shri Gooroo that the Shastras had ordained that all dwellers upon the soil of a Raja should yield of their increase a tenth, at least, whether of fruit, or of cattle, of genius, or of devotion; and since the religious merit of the ascetic had so wonderfully increased, by his long meditation within the Raja's lands, he could not consistently refuse to impart to the Raja a measure of his acquired excellence, by condescending to accept some small gift from his hands.

Shri Gooroo, pretending to be satisfied by this argument, lifted up one of his fingers, which Gopa Sahir explained to the Raja as signifying that the sage would do him the honour of receiving one rupee. The Raja expressed some mortification that so small a gift only would be accepted, but immediately offered a rupee in a posture of profound reverence, and with his hands joined. Shri Gooroo took the coin, and, turning it from side to side, regarded it, for some moments, with looks of utter contempt. "Call you this a rupee?" said he, angrily; "then it is truly a rupee of the *Kali Youg*. A rupee in the *Trita Youg* was equal to, at least, ten thousand of these. How infallible were the predictions of the Shastras!" So saying, he dropped the coin, as if it were valueless. The Raja felt that he was bound to fulfil the expectation which the Brahmin had formed on acceding to the receipt of the rupee; and expecting that the favour of Heaven would repay him a hundred-fold, he ordered ten thousand rupees to be immediately counted out, as a more worthy offering.

Then, on his knees, receiving a benediction, he returned to his palace; and the two impostors decamped with their booty.

I think it will be scarcely too much to assert, that the Hindoos are more adicted to the marvellous than any other known nation upon earth. Their love of the miraculous, combined with their superstitious credulity, lays them open to every species of imposition, both in action and in relation; no fable is too absurd, no farce too monstrous for their belief. This perchance may be, in a degree, as some have asserted, their natural disposition; but, truly, if there were no predisposition to the marvellous, it would be nothing surprising to see a priest-ridden and idolatrous people reduced to any extremity of mental blindness. Their early historians and poets, knowing the difficulty of moving the attention of a people whose taste had become thus vitiated, vied with each other in the concoction of extravagant improbabilities, and it would really appear that each monstrous absurdity has given birth to a race of absurdities more monstrous than itself; for succeeding writers have outdone their predecessors, by continually adding invention to fable; and the wildest conceptions invariably make the deepest impressions. The whole language of the Hindoos has become a heap of allegories; and hence, truth and fiction are so continually blended, that it is impossible, on any occasion, to say where the one ends and the other commences. Hence, they become an easy and unsuspicious prey to the craft of innumerable adventurers, who make a trade in the marvellous, and ramble over the whole country, enriching themselves by the practice alike of the simplest or the grossest impositions. That great and excellent monarch, Krishnaraia, whose whole heart was bent upon the happiness of his people, laboured with great diligence to discover the well of truth; and although a vast accumulation of prejudice, ignorance, and bigotry, covered the entrance, he succeeded, by the aid of his *buhkski*, the wise and illustrious Apa-ji, in removing much of the obstruction; and ultimately drew many copious draughts from that pure spring.

Upon one occasion, Krishnaraia, having no matter of greater importance before him, put a problem to Apa-ji for solution, in presence of the court; propounding it thus:—

"O! Apa-ji! The words of the wise have declared that the deep waters of the pool of reason are, in most persons, stagnant; even though the surface may be rippled by a passing breeze, or slightly agitated by the fall of a shower—that men in their customs, whether civil or religious, are too apt to follow on in one beaten track, without inquiring the condition of the land to which they are travelling; thus the form of religious usages, or of any conventional customs, being once established, will continue to be heedlessly imitated by the undiscerning multitude, however ridiculous or fatal it may be. I desire that you will prove to me the truth or fallacy of this opinion, and discover to me the justice or absurdity of that trite adage '*Jana Marula, jatra Marula,*' which I understand as implying a question of difficulty, as to whether it is the people or their customs, that are ridiculous?" Apa-ji, with his usual diffidence, begged of his majesty time for the solution of so nice a proposition, promising to return a faithful answer in a few days.

This promise he duly performed; and his answer was a practical answer, comprised in the following history of

THE RAJA, HIS BUHKSHI, AND THE GOATHERD.

After Krishnaraia had imposed the foregoing command upon Apa-ji, he dismissed his *durbar*, and the sage immediately retired to the solitudes of a neighbouring forest, intently occupied in the casting of some project which should afford a signal demonstration of the question referred to him. While thus engaged, by chance he cast his eyes upon a venerable-looking old man, who proved to be his own goatherd, one of low degree and of weak intellect, but of a rough and hardy nature, such as are most of his calling. In a moment, a happy design was suggested to the ready mind of the *buhkshi;* and, calling the goatherd to his presence, he thus addressed him:—"Listen to my words, O Bukri-Walla! for I have need of your faithful service; and, if fully yielded, it shall not go without an ample reward: such, indeed, as shall raise you and all your house to comfort and prosperity: but, if you fail me, rest assured that it would have been far better for you never to have seen the light of day."

"O illustrious Apa-ji! protector of the friendless, friend of the poor, staff of the universe, most potent *buhkshi*," replied the goatherd, "I am an insignificant creature, unworthy of your notice, but your devoted slave. Be pleased to do with me whatsoever you will; my life is in your hands, my heart at your service. Though my years be many, though my hairs be grey, yet am I capable of much labour; if my body be spare, my limbs are powerful, and my courage undiminished. Be pleased to command your slave."

"Hear me, then, O Bukri-Walla! You must immediately cast aside this goatherd's costume, and assume the disguise of a Jogi, or penitent devotee; which character I have cause that you should sustain for a time. Your person is in every way suited for the part. Cast off those rags, bedaub your body over with oil and ashes, rub your lips and jaws with saffron, and colour your hair with turmeric, and upon your forehead paint the sacred symbol *Nama*. In your right hand take a bamboo rod of seven knots, in your left a pitcher of water; and carry with you the skin of an antelope, whereon to sit. So, in every respect, shall you be mistaken for a Jogi. Go then to the great cavern in the side of yonder hill, and seat yourself upon the skin, in the manner of a penitent, whose soul is absorbed in contemplation. Your eyes must be fixed upon the ground, your whole person immoveable, having one hand resting upon the crown of your head, while the other keeps your nostrils closed. Under the penalty of death stir not, whatever may befal you. It may be that the Raja himself, with all his retinue of state and a vast concourse of people, will come to visit you. Should the Raja speak to you, or entreat of you, hold your peace. Should he touch or strike you, remain immoveable; and think of a bag of ten thousand rupees, which I now pledge myself to bestow on you, if your part be well performed."

"Beloved of the stars! most incomprehensible Apa-ji, though the king should pluck every hair from my body, yet shall not even my skin be moved; my contemplation shall be at the bottom of the bag of ten thousand rupees; my insensibility shall be like that of death—hearing nothing, feeling nothing, seeing nothing, saying nothing. I am clay, you are the potter."

Doubtless, the poor goatherd, having spent his whole life in tending his goats, had no ambition to change his occupation for that of a Jogi; he had been more willing to have slain a wolf, or to have encountered a tiger, but the *buhkshi's* will was an absolute law, and the bag of ten thousand rupees a fine stimulus. Forthwith he betook himself to the execution of his task. Apa-ji in the meantime returned to the royal palace, and failed not to attend at the second audience. When all the chiefs were assembled, performing the salaam with marked respect, he thus addressed the Raja :—

"O most powerful and merciful of monarchs! I am the bearer of great news; (be my reward suitable!) and claim pardon for interrupting your wise council. Behold the day has arrived, whereon the gods, delighted with your excellence and innumerable virtues, have chosen to reward you with their extraordinary protection and favour. While I am now speaking, a wonderful prodigy exists within your kingdom, and at no great distance from your royal palace. Within the great cave upon the hill side, a penitent, of inconceivable sanctity, has taken up his abode; having, without doubt, descended from the dwelling-place of the divine Vishnu. Steeped in profound meditation upon the perfections of the great Para-Brahma, he is wholly insensible to all terrestrial objects; taking no other nourishment than the air he breathes. I have had evidence, that none of those objects which affect the senses of ordinary persons, make the slightest impression upon him; in fact, it is apparent that the mortal body alone of this sanctified being exists upon this earth; while his soul, his thoughts, all his affections, are absorbed in divinity. We cannot doubt, but that the gods, in sending him to visit your kingdom, design for you an unequivocal proof, in the eyes of all the world, of their peculiar favour and love, both to you and to your subjects. Be pleased to signify your pleasure."

The Raja and his whole court had listened to Apa-ji throughout with earnest attention, and now remained suspended in deep amazement, and inward joy; but the Raja soon made known his determination to visit the illustrious stranger, with all possible pomp, and to implore his blessing. Ere the sun was in the zenith, the royal procession, with the whole court, attended by the entire army, set forth to the cavern; the royal trumpets sounding in all directions, to make known the object of this ado, and inviting all persons whatsoever to be present. As they drew near the cavern, the numbers swelled on all sides to a vast concourse; such, indeed, as had never before been seen in that country; but the joy of every heart was seen reflected in every face, at the distinguished honour thus put upon their prince by the gods themselves, and at the prospect of wealth and abundance which opened to the view of every one. The Raja, with his glorious suite, had ascended the hill, and now approached the cavern, where the wonderful Jogi sojourned. Already penetrated with religious awe, but upheld by his zeal, the Raja entered the retreat of the holy man, with every demonstration of reverence and submission. There he beheld the object of his veneration, in a remote corner. He paused awhile, and gazed at him in silence. A form like that of a statue, rigid and motionless, was seated upon the sacred skin of the antelope, with a pitcher of holy water on one side, and a bamboo rod of seven knots on the other. Its face was deject, and its eyes fixed vacantly upon the ground. One hand rested upon the crown of its head, the other kept the nostrils closed. The whole figure was apparently as inanimate as the rock beneath it. The Raja breathed quickly with reverential dread. He drew near to the heaven-chosen Jogi, and thrice performed a humble prostration. With a trembling voice he thus addressed it :—

"All-wise and powerful Jogi, now upon the threshold of divinity. Blessed, indeed, be my destiny, which has prolonged my existence to this auspicious day, when I am permitted to enjoy the ineffable felicity of beholding your holy feet. The glory which I acquire, by looking upon your beneficent countenance, infinitely exceeds the public renown which emblazons the great virtues of other men. How have I deserved so distinguished a mark of divine approbation? Surely I can attribute it only to the merits of my ancestors, or to some acceptable work which I may have been enabled to perform in a preceding generation, the memory whereof no longer remains to me. But, however obtained, this glorious hour, in which I first behold the lustre of your hallowed feet, is by far the happiest of my existence. Henceforth, I can have nothing to covet in this world. It is sufficient for any mortal to have seen that inspired form; for so beatific a vision will assuredly blot out the sins of all beholders, committed either in this or in any preceding generation. Now do I esteem myself as pure as the sacred stream of the Ganges, and have nothing more to desire upon earth."

The profound Jogi received this flattering speech from the royal tongue, without manifesting the slightest emotion; every muscle remained inflexible. All the spectators were amazed, and could only admire, in silent eloquence, the wonderful sanctity and holy abstraction of that being, who could receive the submissive addresses of their renowned Raja, without even deigning to cast a glance of approbation towards him. Well might it be said, thought they, that the empty frame of the venerable Jogi dwelt upon the earth, while his soul, his thoughts, all his affections, had been re-united to Para-Brahma! Krishnaraia continued to gaze in admiration, and frequently essayed, by renewed adulation and compliment, to gain but a single look, or breath of approval, from the saintly Jogi; but that wonderful being remained absorbed in contemplation of visions extra-mundane. At length, when importunity and perseverance appeared alike ineffectual, the Raja was about to take his leave; but the *buhkshi* Apa-ji interposed:—

"Most gracious monarch," said he, "the first sight of this holy personage, who will henceforward become the object of extraordinary veneration to the whole world, is, surely an event never to be forgotten, and should require no memento; still, as you have not yet succeeded in obtaining his special notice and blessing, it will, perchance, be well to seize the present opportunity of securing some relic of his inestimably precious person; if it were no more than one of the hairs which you see growing so profusely about him."

Krishnaraia being greatly delighted at this thoughtful suggestion, commended his *buhkshi*, and immediately advancing with suitable awe, plucked a hair from the shaggy breast of the Jogi. He pressed it to his lips, and kissed it fervently, saying—"I will enshrine it in an amulet of pure gold, set with the most costly gems; and I will always wear it suspended from my neck, as the most precious of my ornaments. It shall be an heir-loom in our house, a talisman against all evil, the source of perpetual prosperity."

Now the ministers and courtiers who attended the Raja could not refrain from possessing themselves of a similar treasure; and each plucked a hair from the breast of the meditative Jogi, to be preserved as a sacred relic for future generations. Likewise the vast multitude who now filled the plain, hearing, by degrees, what had been passing in the cave, thronged around the entrance, burning with anxiety to secure a similar advantage; and when the Raja had departed, each plucked his treasure, until scarce a hair was left upon the tortured goatherd—the sanctified penitent. But he endured all with utter indifference; nor winced, nor sighed, nor faltered in his steadfast gaze.

Upon his return to the royal palace, the good Raja Krishnaraia related to his eager wives the whole history of his adventures, and showed them the wonderful relic which he had stolen from the person of the godlike Jogi. They listened and beheld, with inconceivable curiosity and delight; and implored, with womanly importunity, that, on so extraordinary an occasion, their beloved prince and master would be pleased to release them from the restrictions of custom, and permit them to make a visit to the famous recluse; or, at least, that he might be brought into their presence, so that they might each pluck a hair (if any remained) from his body with their own hands. Krishnaraia of course raised many difficulties in the way of these unconventional desires; but, being hotly driven from objection to objection, he at last consented to gratify them; and for the purpose of doing due honour to the Jogi, he again ordered out his entire retinue, with all his force of horse and foot, to serve as an escort. On their arrival at the cavern, which was still surrounded by a large concourse of persons, who had not yet been able to procure a hair, the chiefs dismounted, and prostrating themselves before the Jogi, unfolded their mission. Then, receiving no token, they took up the motionless penitent in their arms, with great reverence, and placed him in a superb new palanquin of state, in the same posture as that in which they had found him. The Jogi was thus conducted through the principal streets of the city, attended by an innumerable host of people, who made the heavens resound with the impassioned fervour of their joyful acclamations. Poor goatherd! he sat immoveable, still sustaining his assumed character with admirable fortitude, although he was, in truth, faint with hunger, and the entire surface of his body had become suffused with blood, by the perpetual plucking of the hairs. Alas! he had little enjoyment in his triumphant honours, and the bag of ten thousand rupees in perspective would have been insufficient to have restrained him from betraying himself and his master, had it not been for the fear of a cruel punishment. In his own mind, he could not but continually repeat,—"Why should I be thus compelled to carry on this villanous trick, in the midst of pain and misery? Would that I were once more in company with my poor deserted goats, who may, ere this, have become a prey to the wild beasts. I would rather encounter a tiger, than be persecuted by this noisy multitude. Had I been with my flock, I should have been blessed with three hearty meals; whereas, now, I have fasted well-nigh to death, and know not when I may be relieved."

While these comfortless thoughts were passing through the mind of the counterfeit Jogi, the procession arrived at the royal palace; and being put down in a magnificent apartment, he immediately received a visit from the princesses. These beautiful young women prostrated themselves, one by one, at his feet; and, after a pause of silent admiration, each of them would pluck a hair, to be set like the Raja's in a jewel, and ever worn as a charm. But it was no easy matter to find one; the very pate was absolutely bald: and it was only by carefully exploring the folds and wrinkles, which a venerable beard had lately covered, that each lady could be accommodated with a relic. At last they concluded their devout visit and retired, leaving the Jogi still in his attitude of profound meditation, from which, however, the Raja at last relieved him, by ordering all the doors to be closed, that he might remain undisturbed during the night.

When all the inhabitants of the palace had retired, Apa-ji introduced himself to the poor goatherd by a secret passage, and taking him to his own apartment, he rewarded him with a sumptuous banquet, and an earnest of his ten thousand rupees; bidding him return home, and, with the dawn of day, to resume his accustomed calling, and to maintain a profound secrecy concerning the fraud, until he should receive permission to speak. Poor Bukri-Walla! he did not wait a second bidding, but got him quickly to his humble home, resolved never again to act the Jogi. Early on the next morning, Krishnaraia went to renew his solicitations to the venerable penitent; but, alas! he found him not; he had vanished, or had mysteriously conveyed himself through the closed doors. The advent and departure were equally wonderful; and the veneration of all men was augmented. How truly felicitous were all those who had secured a relic! The whole affair continued, for many days, to be the only topic of the court, the city, and the country; but it gradually grew stale, and at last was only occasionally remembered, like any other antiquated miracle. However, in the interim, the *buhkshi's* goatherd had found great treasure, and he, and all his family, dwelt in comparative wealth.

Some months after these events, Krishnaraia was reminded of the old proverb,—" *Jana Marula, jatra Marula;*" and turning immediately to the *buhkshi*, he inquired if he had yet made up his mind touching that familiar saying. Apa-ji, who, in truth, had only waited for such an opportunity, first obtained the Raja's permission to speak without reserve, deprecating anger, and then, to the astonished court, thus declared himself:—" Incomparable sovereign! your own actions a few months since furnished a full and striking demonstration of this problem, when you condescended to visit the cavern in yonder hill, and paid your reverence, you and all your people, to the impostor who sojourned there. You have graciously given me permission to speak my whole mind with impunity; and now, know all men, that the sanctified Jogi was no other than the humble goatherd of your majesty's more humble slave, Apa-ji; a being so useless and uncultivated, as to approach to utter stupidity. Such is the personage whom you and your court, upon the strength of my naked assertion, have loaded with honours almost divine, and have elevated to the rank of a saint. The credulous multitude, without thought or question, blindly followed your example; and, without any knowledge of the object of its adoration, ran with you into the excess of fanatical zeal, in favour of an abject goatherd, low-born, uneducated, well-nigh a fool. From this convincing instance all the world must be satisfied that conventional institutions are matters of example and habit, varnished over with prejudice; and that it is not so much the absurd usages of any country which should incur our ridicule, as the persons who blindly practise them."

Krishnaraia, like a wise sovereign, took in good part the pointed and ingenious conceit which Apa-ji had so boldly adopted, to enlighten his mind upon a matter so important and abstruse; and he beheld his excellent *buhkshi* with renewed favour, after he had recovered from his surprise. Moreover, he continued ever after to regard him as his most faithful subject and friend. Yet, without doubt, should another goatherd have been presented to him in the disguise of a Jogi, the farce would have been repeated.

THE END.